First World War

and Army of Occupation

War Diary

France, Belgium and Germany

2 DIVISION
Divisional Troops
Royal Army Medical Corps
4 Field Ambulance
1 January 1915 - 28 February 1915

WO95/1336/2

The Naval & Military Press Ltd
www.nmarchive.com
Published in association with The National Archives

Published by

The Naval & Military Press Ltd

Unit 10 Ridgewood Industrial Park,

Uckfield, East Sussex,

TN22 5QE England

Tel: +44 (0) 1825 749494

www.naval-military-press.com

www.nmarchive.com

This diary has been reprinted in facsimile from the original. Any imperfections are inevitably reproduced and the quality may fall short of modern type and cartographic standards.

Contents

Document type	Place/Title	Date From	Date To
Heading	Cover For Documents. Nature Of Enclosures.No 4 Field Ambulance		
Miscellaneous	4 Field Ambulance	01/01/1915	01/01/1915
War Diary	Bethune	01/01/1915	02/01/1915
Miscellaneous	No 4 Field Ambulance	02/01/1915	02/01/1915
War Diary	Bethune	03/01/1915	03/01/1915
Miscellaneous	No 4 Field Ambulance	03/01/1915	03/01/1915
War Diary	Bethune	04/01/1915	04/01/1915
Miscellaneous	No 4 Field Ambulance	04/01/1915	04/01/1915
War Diary	Bethune	05/01/1915	05/01/1915
Miscellaneous	No 4 Field Ambulance	05/01/1915	05/01/1915
War Diary	Bethune	06/01/1915	06/01/1915
Miscellaneous	No 4 Field Ambulance	06/01/1915	06/01/1915
War Diary	Bethune	07/01/1915	07/01/1915
Miscellaneous	No 4 Field Ambulance	07/01/1915	07/01/1915
War Diary	Bethune	08/01/1915	08/01/1915
Miscellaneous	No 4 Field Ambulance	08/01/1915	08/01/1915
War Diary	Bethune	09/01/1915	09/01/1915
Miscellaneous	No 4 Field Ambulance	09/01/1915	09/01/1915
War Diary	Bethune	10/01/1915	10/01/1915
Miscellaneous	No. 4 Field Ambulance	10/01/1915	10/01/1915
War Diary	Bethune	11/01/1915	11/01/1915
Miscellaneous	No 4 Field Ambulance	11/01/1915	11/01/1915
War Diary	Bethune	12/01/1915	13/01/1915
Miscellaneous	O.O. No 4 Field Ambulance	05/03/1916	05/03/1916
War Diary	Bethune	14/01/1915	24/01/1915
Miscellaneous	Emile Leman Notaire Bethune		
War Diary	Bethune	24/01/1915	25/01/1915
War Diary	Robecq	25/01/1915	28/01/1915
Miscellaneous	O C Field Ambulance	29/01/1915	29/01/1915
War Diary	Robecq	29/01/1915	31/01/1915
Miscellaneous	O C 4 Field Ambulance	02/01/1915	02/01/1915
Miscellaneous	Copy of Message G 826 d/6-1-15 from 2nd Division Begin	06/01/1915	06/01/1915
Miscellaneous	4th Field Ambulance		
Miscellaneous	O C 4th 5th Field Ambulance	29/01/1915	29/01/1915
Miscellaneous	2 Division R.A.M.C. Operation Orders by Colonel M.P.G. Holt D.S.O. A.D.M.S.	31/01/1915	31/01/1915
Miscellaneous	After Orders	31/01/1915	31/01/1915
Miscellaneous	Operations		
Diagram etc	Diagram		
Heading	No 4 Field Ambulance Vol VII		
Miscellaneous	16 Op.		
War Diary	Robecq	01/02/1915	01/02/1915
Miscellaneous	No 4 Field Ambulance	01/02/1915	01/02/1915
War Diary	Bethune	01/02/1915	01/02/1915
Miscellaneous	No 4 Field Ambulance	02/02/1915	02/02/1915
War Diary	Bethune	02/02/1915	02/02/1915
Miscellaneous	No 4 Field Ambulance	03/02/1915	03/02/1915
War Diary	Bethune	03/02/1915	03/02/1915

Miscellaneous	No 4 Field Ambulance	04/02/1915	04/02/1915
War Diary	Bethune	04/02/1915	04/02/1915
Miscellaneous	No 4 Field Ambulance	05/02/1915	05/02/1915
War Diary	Bethune	05/02/1915	05/02/1915
Miscellaneous	No 4 Field Ambulance	06/02/1915	06/02/1915
War Diary	Bethune	06/02/1915	06/02/1915
Miscellaneous	No 4 Field Ambulance	07/02/1915	07/02/1915
War Diary	Bethune	07/02/1915	07/02/1915
Miscellaneous	No 4 Fd Ambce	08/02/1915	08/02/1915
War Diary	Bethune	08/02/1915	08/02/1915
Miscellaneous	No 4 Field Ambulance	09/02/1915	09/02/1915
War Diary	Bethune	09/02/1915	09/02/1915
Miscellaneous	No 4 Field Ambulance	10/02/1915	10/02/1915
War Diary	Bethune	10/02/1915	10/02/1915
Miscellaneous	No. 4 Field Ambulance	11/02/1915	11/02/1915
War Diary	Bethune	11/02/1915	11/02/1915
Miscellaneous	No 4 Field Ambulance	12/02/1915	12/02/1915
War Diary	Bethune	12/02/1915	12/02/1915
Miscellaneous	No 4 Field Ambulance	13/02/1915	13/02/1915
War Diary	Bethune	13/02/1915	13/02/1915
Miscellaneous	No. 4 Field Ambulance	14/02/1915	14/02/1915
Miscellaneous	ADMS 2nd Division	14/02/1915	14/02/1915
War Diary	Bethune	14/02/1915	14/02/1915
Miscellaneous	No 4 Field Ambulance	15/02/1915	15/02/1915
War Diary	Bethune	15/02/1915	15/02/1915
Miscellaneous	No. 4 Field Ambulance	16/02/1915	16/02/1915
War Diary	Bethune	16/02/1915	16/02/1915
Miscellaneous	No 4 Field Ambulance	17/02/1915	17/02/1915
War Diary	Bethune	17/02/1915	17/02/1915
Miscellaneous	No 4 Field Ambulance	18/02/1915	18/02/1915
War Diary	Bethune	18/02/1915	18/02/1915
Miscellaneous	No 4 Field Ambulance	19/02/1915	19/02/1915
War Diary	Bethune	19/02/1915	19/02/1915
Miscellaneous	No 4 Field Ambulance	20/02/1915	20/02/1915
War Diary	Bethune	20/02/1915	20/02/1915
Miscellaneous	No 4 Field Ambulance	21/02/1915	21/02/1915
War Diary	Bethune	21/02/1915	21/02/1915
Miscellaneous	No 4 Field Ambulance	22/02/1915	22/02/1915
War Diary	Bethune	22/02/1915	22/02/1915
Miscellaneous	No. 4 Field Ambulance	23/02/1915	23/02/1915
War Diary	Bethune	23/02/1915	23/02/1915
Miscellaneous	No. 4 Field Ambulance	24/02/1915	24/02/1915
War Diary	Bethune	24/02/1915	24/02/1915
Miscellaneous	No 4 Field Ambulance	25/02/1915	25/02/1915
Miscellaneous	To Os.C 4,5,6 F Ambs G Staff And A.D.M.S 1st Divn	24/02/1915	24/02/1915
Miscellaneous	Oc 4/5/6 Field Ambulance	24/02/1915	24/02/1915
War Diary	Bethune	25/02/1915	25/02/1915
Miscellaneous	No. 4 Field Ambulance	26/02/1915	26/02/1915
War Diary		26/02/1915	26/02/1915
Miscellaneous	No 4 Field Ambulance	27/02/1915	27/02/1915
War Diary	Bethune	27/02/1915	27/02/1915
Miscellaneous	No 4 Field Ambulance	28/02/1915	28/02/1915
War Diary	Bethune	28/02/1915	28/02/1915

(6414) Wt. W3905/P1607 2,500,000 7/18 McA & W Ltd (E 3591) Forms W3091/4.

Army Form W.3091.

Cover for Documents.

Nature of Enclosures.

No. 4 Field Amb

Notes, or Letters written.

19

No 4 Field Ambulance.

Capacity :- Officers 8
Other Ranks

	Officers		Other Ranks	
	Sick	Wound	Sick	Wounded
In occupation	2	-	116	9
Lying	-	-	-	-
Sitting	-	-	6	
Walking	-	-	-	-
Unfit to move	-	-	-	-
Fit for evacuation	2	-	110	9

[illegible]
Capt RAMC
OC 4 Fd Amb

11-30 am
1. 1. 15.

D D M S
1st Army Corps

[illegible] Field Ambulance

Capacity: Officers 8
Other Ranks 280

	Officers		Other Ranks	
	Sick	Wounded	Sick	Wounded
In occupation	3	-	175	14
Lying	-	-	4	
Sitting	-	-	6	4
Walking	-	-	-	-
Unfit to move	-	-	-	3
Not for evacuation	3	-	165	7.

P.A. Lloyd Jones.
Capt RAMC
OC 2 Fd Amb

5.30 pm
1.1.15

DDMS
1st Army Corps

Instructions regarding War Diaries and Intelligence Summaries are contained in F. S. Regs., Part II. and the Staff Manual respectively. Title pages will be prepared in manuscript.

WAR DIARY
or
~~INTELLIGENCE SUMMARY.~~
(Erase heading not required.)

Army Form C. 2118.

Hour, Date, Place	Summary of Events and Information	Remarks and references to Appendices
January 1st/15. BETHUNE	A convalescent Depot opened at St OMER for reception of cases likely to be fit for duty within a week. 1 case admitted, wounded back, left kidney implicated No of sick = 81 No of Cases evacuated = 61.	PALJ.

(73989) W4141—463. 400,000. 9/14. H.&J.Ltd. Forms/C. 2118/10.

Army Form C. 2118.

WAR DIARY
or
~~INTELLIGENCE SUMMARY.~~
(Erase heading not required.)

Instructions regarding War Diaries and Intelligence Summaries are contained in F. S. Regs., Part II and the Staff Manual respectively. Title pages will be prepared in manuscript.

Hour, Date, Place	Summary of Events and Information	Remarks and references to Appendices
January 2nd/15 BETHUNE	No of Sick = 82 No. of Cases evacuated = 20	PHG.

(73989) W4141—463. 400,000. 9/14. H.&J.Ltd. Forms/C. 2118/10.

No. [illegible] Field Ambulance

Capacity for Officers 8
Other Ranks 2[illegible]0

	Officers		Other Ranks	
	Sick	Wounded	Sick	Wounded
In occupation	3	–	18	18
Lying	–	–	–	–
Sitting	–	–	6	7
Walking	–	–	–	–
Unfit to move	–	–	–	3
Ready for evacuation	3	–	16	8

7.30 am
2-1-15

[signature]
Captain R.A.M.C.
O.C. [illegible] Fd. Amb.

D.D.M.S.
[illegible] Army Corps

6 Field Ambulance

Capacity - Officers 8
Other ranks 180

	Officers		Other Ranks	
	Sick	Wounded	Sick	Wounded
In occupation	3	-	165	12
Lying			8	-
Sitting			11	-
Walking			-	-
Unfit to move			-	4
Fit for evacuation	3	-	146	8

P.A. Lloyd Jones.
Capt. R.A.M.C.
O.C. 6th Fd. Amb.

11.45 a.m.
2.1.15.

D.D.M.S.
1st Army Corps.

No 4 Field Ambulance

Capacity: Officers 8
Other Ranks 280

	Officers		Other Ranks	
	Sick	Wounded	Sick	Wounded
In occupation	4	1	141	23
Lying			8	3
Sitting			18	3
Walking	1			
Unfit to move				5
Not for evacuation	3	1	115	12.

R. Ashton Jones
Capt RAM Corps
OC No 4 Fd Amb

5.45 pm
2.1.18

DDMS
1st Army Corps

Instructions regarding War Diaries and Intelligence Summaries are contained in F. S. Regs., Part II. and the Staff Manual respectively. Title pages will be prepared in manuscript.

WAR DIARY

or

~~INTELLIGENCE SUMMARY.~~

(*Erase heading not required.*)

Army Form C. 2118.

Hour, Date, Place	Summary of Events and Information	Remarks and references to Appendices
January 3rd/15 BETHUNE	No of Sick - 50 No of Cases evacuated 73	PAG.

(73989) W4141—463. 400,000. 9/14. H.&J.Ltd. Forms/C. 2118/10.

No 4 Field Ambulance

Capacity : Officers 8
Other Ranks 250

	Officers		Other Ranks	
	Sick	Wounded	Sick	Wounded
In accommodation	5	1	148	21
Lying	—	—	9	9
Sitting	—	1	4	5
Walking	—	—	—	-
Unfit to move	—	—	—	-
Fit for evacuation	5	—	132	15

30 A.m
1 – 15
D.M.S.
1st Army Corps.

P.A. Lloyd Jones
Capt R.A.M.C.
O.C. No 4 Field Ambce

No. 4 Field Ambulance

Capacity:- Officers 8
Other Ranks 280

	Officers		Other [illegible]	
	Sick	Wounded	Sick	[illegible]
In occupation	4	1	143	28
Lying	1		8*	7
Sitting			18	4
Walking				
Unfit to move				3
Not for evacuation	3	1	119	14

* One case to be lying (suspected Enteric)

[illegible]
Capt AAMC
for O.C. 4th Fd Amb.

11.30 a.m.
3. 1. 15

D.D.M.S.
1st Army Corps

No 4 Field Ambulance

Capacity ~~[illegible]~~ Officers 8
Other ranks 280

	Officers		Other Ranks	
	Sick	Wounded	Sick	Wounded
In occupation	3	7	184	31
Lying	1	1	98*	10
Sitting				4
Walking			23	
Unfit to move				2
Fit for evacuation	4	·	155	15

* One case lying (suspected Enteric).

T. S. [illegible]

Capt. R.A.M.C.

O.C. No 4 Fd. Amb.

5 30 pm
3. 1. 15

D.D.M.S.
1st Army Corps

Instructions regarding War Diaries and Intelligence Summaries are contained in F. S. Regs., Part II. and the Staff Manual respectively. Title pages will be prepared in manuscript.

WAR DIARY

or

~~INTELLIGENCE SUMMARY.~~

(Erase heading not required.)

Army Form C. 2118.

Hour, Date, Place	Summary of Events and Information	Remarks and references to Appendices
January 4th/15	No of sick = 67	PAJG.
BETHUNE	No of cases evacuated = 20.	

(73989) W4141—463. 400,000. 9/14. H.&J.Ltd. Forms/C. 2118/10.

No 4 Field Ambulance

Total Capacity: Officers 8.
Other Ranks 280.

	Officers		Other Ranks	
	Sick	Wounded	Sick	Wounded
In occupation	5	1	202	34
Lying	1		7	12
Sitting	1	1	43	7
Walking	–	–	–	–
Unfit to move	–	–	–	–
Not for evacuation	3	–	152	15

7.30 am.
4-1-15.

L S Blackwell [?]

DDMS
1st Army Corps.

Captn RAMC
O.C. No 4 Field Amb[ulan]ce

[illegible] Field Ambulance

Capacity – Officers 8
Other Ranks 2[illegible]

	Officers		Other Ranks	
	Sick	Wounded	Sick	Wounded
In occupation	2	-	146	14
Lying			—	1
Sitting			2	1
Walking			1	—
Unfit to move			—	3
Not for evacuation	2	-	144	12

11.30 p.m.
4.1.15

Capt. [illegible]
O.C. 4 Fd. Amb.

D.D.M.S.
1st Army Corps

No 4 Fd Ambulance

Capacity :- Officers 8
Other Ranks 2[illegible]

	Officers		Other Ranks	
	Sick	Wounded	Sick	Wounded
In occupation	2	–	169	21
Lying	–	–	–	2
Sitting	–	–	2	1
Walking	–	–	–	–
Unfit to move	–	–	–	3
Fit for evacuation	2	–	167	15

J S [illegible]

5.30 p.m.
4.1.15

Capt RAMC
O.C. No 4 Fd Amb.

DDMS
1st Army Corps

Instructions regarding War Diaries and Intelligence Summaries are contained in F. S. Regs., Part II. and the Staff Manual respectively. Title pages will be prepared in manuscript.

WAR DIARY
or
INTELLIGENCE ~~SUMMARY~~.
(*Erase heading not required.*)

Army Form C. 2118.

Hour, Date, Place	Summary of Events and Information	Remarks and references to Appendices
January 5th/15 BETHUNE	Visit from D.D.M.S. 1st Army and ADMS 2nd Div. Office of the D.D.M.S. removed. Hospital getting congested owing to evacuations being slow. Sick evacuation return now sent to No 1 Clearing Hospital instead of D.D.M.S. No 6 Field Ambulance opened Convalescent Home. No of Sick 84 No of cases evacuated = 109	PRG

(73989) W4141—463. 400,000. 9/14. H.&J.Ltd. Forms/C. 2118/10.

No 4 Field Ambulance

Capacity Officers 8
Other Ranks 280

	Officers		Other Ranks	
	Sick	Wnd^d^	Sick	Wnd
In occupation	3	–	173	27
Lying	–	–	–	5
Sitting	–	–	9	5
Walking	–	–	–	–
Unfit to move	–	–	1	2
Fit for evacuation	3	–	163	15

7 [illegible]
5-1-15

DDMS.
1st Army Corps

J. S. [illegible]

Capt R.A.M.C.
O.C. No 4 Field Amb^ce^

[illegible] Field Ambulance

Capacity: Officers 8
Other Ranks 280

	Officers		Other ranks	
	Sick	Wounded	Sick	Wounded
In accommodation	3	–	139	1[illegible]
Lying	–		2*	2
Sitting	–	–	5	1
Walking	–	–	–	–
Unfit to move	–	–	–	–
Not for evacuation	3	–	142	12

* One case suspected Enteric (lying)

[illegible]

11.30 a.m. [illegible] Capt RAMC
[illegible] Cmd [illegible] Amb

[illegible]
[illegible]

No 4 Field Ambulance

Capacity: Officers 8
Other Ranks 280

	Officers		Other Ranks	
	Sick	Wounded	Sick	Wounded
In occupation	6	2	182	24
Lying	-	-	4	4
Sitting	-	2	19	3
Walking	-	-	-	-
Unfit to move	-	-	-	3
Not for evacuation	6	-	159	14

[illegible]

5 - 30 p.m.
5. 1. 16

Capt RAMC
O.C. 4th Fld Amb.

DDMS
1st Army Corps

Instructions regarding War Diaries and Intelligence Summaries are contained in F. S. Regs., Part II. and the Staff Manual respectively. Title pages will be prepared in manuscript.

WAR DIARY
or
~~INTELLIGENCE SUMMARY~~.
(*Erase heading not required.*)

Army Form C. 2118.

Hour, Date, Place	Summary of Events and Information	Remarks and references to Appendices
January 6th/15. BETHUNE.	Visit from A.D.M.S. Closed one Officers' dressing station, and no more Officers admitted. Notified 4th (Guards) Infantry Brigade to this effect No of Sick. 70 No of Cases evacuated = 25	PHG.

(73989) W4141—463. 400,000. 9/14. H.&J.Ltd. Forms/C. 2118/10.

[illegible] Field Ambulance

Capacity: Officers 8
Other Ranks 280

	Officers		Other Ranks	
	[illegible]	Wounded	Sick	Wounded
In occupation	3	1	182	17
[illegible]			–	–
[illegible]			3	–
[illegible]			–	–
[illegible]			–	5
[illegible]	3	1	179	12

P.A. Lloyd Jones.
Capt RAMC
[illegible] Field Amb

[illegible]
1918

No 4 Field Ambulance

Capacity - Officers 8
Other Ranks 280

	Officers		Other Ranks	
	Sick	Wounded	Sick	Wounded
In occupation	4		224	20
Lying			1	3
Sitting			13	1
Walking				
Unfit to move				4
Fit for evacuation	4		210	12

5.45 pm
6.1.15

R A Lloyd Jones
Capt RAMC
OC No 4 Fd Amb

D D M S
1st Corps

No 4 Field Ambulance

Capacity: Officers 8
Other ranks 280

	Officers		Other Ranks	
	Sick	Wound^d	Sick	Wounded
Now occupation	5	2	210	38
Lying	–	–	7	12
Sitting	1	2	23	8
Walking	–	–	–	–
Unfit to move	–	–	1	4
Not for evacuation	4	–	179	14

7.30 am
6. 1. 15

J. S. Dunn[illegible]
Capt RAMC
OC No 4 Field Amb^ce

Instructions regarding War Diaries and Intelligence Summaries are contained in F. S. Regs., Part II. and the Staff Manual respectively. Title pages will be prepared in manuscript.

WAR DIARY
or
~~INTELLIGENCE SUMMARY.~~
(Erase heading not required.)

Army Form C. 2118.

Hour, Date, Place	Summary of Events and Information	Remarks and references to Appendices
January 7th/15 BETHUNE	No of Sick - 73. No of cases evacuated. - 59	[illegible]

(73989) W4141—463. 400,000. 9/14. H.&J.Ltd. Forms/C. 2118/10.

No 4 Field Ambulance

Capacity Officers 8
Other Ranks 280

	Officers		Other Ranks	
	Sick	Wnd^d	Sick	Wnd^d
No in occupation	4	2	169	94
Lying	–	–	1	7
Sitting	–	–	20	4
Walking	–	–	–	.
Unfit to move	–	–	1	2
Not for Evacuation	4	2	147	81

O.C.
No 7 Clearing Hosp^l.
7.30 am
7-1-15.

P.A. Lloyd Jones
Capt RAMC
O.C. No 4 Field Amb^ce.

No 4 Field Ambulance

Capacity :- Officers 8
Other Ranks 280

	Sick Officers		Other Ranks	
	Sick	Wounded	Sick	Wounded
In occupation	4	2	229	24
Lying			2	7
Sitting			23	4
Walking				
Unfit to move				3
Not for evacuation	4	2	204	13

11.30 a.m.
4.1.15

for Capt. Ramsell(?)
O.C. No 4 Fd Amb

O.C. No 1 Clearing Hospl

No 4 Field Ambulance

Capacity Officers 8.
Other Ranks 280

	Officers		Other Ranks	
	Sick	Wnd	Sick	Wnd
In occupation	4	3	*176	22
Lying	-	-	1	2
Sitting	-	-		5
Walking	-	-	-	-
Unfit to move	-	-	-	-
Not for evacuation	4	3.	175	15

* Suspected Enteric

5 30 pm
=
7-1-15

OC No 1 Clearing Hospl

R. A. Lloyd Jones.
Captn RAMC
OC No 4 Field Ambce

Army Form C. 2118.

Instructions regarding War Diaries and Intelligence Summaries are contained in F. S. Regs., Part II. and the Staff Manual respectively. Title pages will be prepared in manuscript.

WAR DIARY

or

~~INTELLIGENCE SUMMARY.~~

(Erase heading not required.)

Hour, Date, Place	Summary of Events and Information	Remarks and references to Appendices
January 8th/15. BETHUNE	Corpl. Gardner R.A.M.C. transferred to No 6 Field Ambulance for duty. No of cases evacuated = 113	PHG.

(9 26 6) W257—976 100,000 4/12 H W V 79/3298

No. 4 Field Ambulance.

Capacity Officers 8
Other Ranks 280

	Officers		Other Ranks	
	Sick	Wnd.	Sick	Wnd.
No. in occupation	4	3	214	26
Lying	–	–	2[x]	3
Sitting	–	–	3	6
Walking	–	–	–	–
Unfit to move	–	–	2	2
Not for evacuation	4	3	207	15

x Includes one case suspected Enteric

O.C. No. 1 Clearing Hospl.

8 a.m.
8-1-15

P. A. Lloyd Jones
Captn RAMC
O.C. No. 4 Field Ambulance

A.W. W.L. 8 Field Ambulance

On Duty – Officers 8
Other Ranks 280

	Officers		Other Ranks	
	Sick	Wounded	Sick	Wounded
In occupation	4	3	223	23
Lying			1	1
Sitting		1	4	
Walking				
Unfit to move				5
Not for evacuation	4	2	115	15

3-30 p.m.
~~11-30 a.m.~~
8. 1. 15

P. A. Lloyd Jones
Capt. R.A.M.C.
O.C. No. 8 Fd. Amb.

O.C. No. 1 Clearing Hosp.

Army Form C. 2118.

Instructions regarding War Diaries and Intelligence Summaries are contained in F. S. Regs., Part II. and the Staff Manual respectively. Title pages will be prepared in manuscript.

WAR DIARY
or
~~INTELLIGENCE SUMMARY~~.

(*Erase heading not required.*)

Hour, Date, Place	Summary of Events and Information	Remarks and references to Appendices
January 9th/15 BETHUNE	No of Sick = 84 No of cases evacuated = 65	PHJ

(73989) W4141—463. 400,000. 9/14. H.&J.Ltd. Forms/C. 2118/10.

No 4 Field Ambulance

Capacity Officers 8.
Other Ranks 280

	Officers		Other Ranks.	
	Sick	Wndd	Sick	Wndd.
No in occupation	2	3	234	27
Lying	–	–	2	2
Sitting	–	1	8	3
Walking	–	–	–	–
Unfit to move	–	–	1	4
Not for evacuation	2	2	223	18

O.C. No. 1 Clearing Hospital.

9 am.
9/1/15

P. A. Lloyd Jones
Capt. RAMC.
OC 4th Fd. Ambce.

No 4 Field Ambulance

Capacity Officers 5.
Other Ranks 280.

	Officers		Other Ranks	
	Sick	Wnd	Sick	Wnd
No in occupation	1	2	244	28
Lying			2	2
Sitting			17	8
Walking				
Unfit to move				6
Not for evacuation	1	2	225	14

5.30 pm
9-1-15

P.A. Lloyd Jones.
Capt RAMC
O.C. No 4 Field Ambulance

O.C. No 1 Clearing Hosp.

Instructions regarding War Diaries and Intelligence Summaries are contained in F. S. Regs., Part II. and the Staff Manual respectively. Title pages will be prepared in manuscript.

WAR DIARY
or
~~INTELLIGENCE SUMMARY~~.
(*Erase heading not required.*)

Army Form C. 2118.

Hour, Date, Place	Summary of Events and Information	Remarks and references to Appendices
January 10th/15. BETHUNE	No. of Sick = 91 No of cases evacuated = 50	DHG.

(73989) W4141—463. 400,000. 9/14. H.&J.Ltd. Forms/C. 2118/10.

No. 4 Field Ambulance.

Capacity – Officers 5
Other Ranks. 280

	Officers		Other Ranks	
	Sick	Wnd.	Sick	Wnd.
In occupation	1	2	272	31
Lying	–	–	3	2
Sitting	–	–	X 36	14
Walking	–	–	–	–
Unfit to move	–	–	–	–
Not fit for evacn.	1	2	233	15

X 4 Suspected Enteric carriers.

To O.C. No. 1 Clearing Hospital
[illegible] 14/1/15

[illegible signature]
Capt. R.A.M.C.
O.C. No. 4 Field Amb.

No 4 Field Ambulance

Capacity :- Officers 8.
Other Ranks 280.

	Officers		Other Ranks	
	Sick	Wounded	Sick	Wounded
In occupation	1	2	173	22
Lying			3	1
Sitting			22x	3
Walking			–	–
Unfit to move			–	5
Fit for evacuation	1	2	148	13.

x four suspected Enteric Carriers

P. A. Lloyd Jones

Capt RAMC
O.C. No 4 Fd Amb

7.15 p m
? 1. 15

C
No 1 Clearing Hospl

Army Form C. 2118.

WAR DIARY

or

~~INTELLIGENCE SUMMARY.~~

(*Erase heading not required.*)

Instructions regarding War Diaries and Intelligence Summaries are contained in F. S. Regs., Part II. and the Staff Manual respectively. Title pages will be prepared in manuscript.

Hour, Date, Place	Summary of Events and Information	Remarks and references to Appendices
January 11th/15 BETHUNE	Department started under Captn Boyce for clearing clothes and boots, also for drying and softening boots. The boots are dried on wooden shelves surrounding the stove in packstore and are softened in warm lubricating oil Boot-issuing department started for issuing every man who returns to trenches & has defective boots, with a new pair properly softened; also a size too large ~~so that~~ he can wear the two pairs of socks with which he is provided. No 5249 Pte Jones RAMC. Joined for duty. No of Sick = 64 No of Cases evacuated = 157	PHG.

(73989) W4141—463. 400,000. 9/14. H.&J.Ltd. Forms/C. 2118/10.

No 4. Field Ambulance.

Capacity - Officers 5
Other Ranks 280

	Officers		Other Ranks	
	Sick	Wound	Sick	Wound
No in occupation	1	2	178	31
Lying	–	–	2[x]	3
Sitting	–	–	28[ø]	6
Walking	–	–	–	–
Unfit to move	–	–	–	–
Not for evacuation	1	2	148	22

x 1 Suspected Enteric
ø 4 " " Carriers
2 M.M.P. are accompanying as escort to
6 Self Inflicted Wound cases.

To O.C. No. 1 Clearing Hospital.
9 am 11/1/15.

R A Lloyd Jones

Capt. RAMC
O.C. 4th Fd. Ambulance.

Army Form C. 2118.

WAR DIARY
or
~~INTELLIGENCE SUMMARY.~~
(Erase heading not required.)

Instructions regarding War Diaries and Intelligence Summaries are contained in F. S. Regs., Part II. and the Staff Manual respectively. Title pages will be prepared in manuscript.

Hour, Date, Place	Summary of Events and Information	Remarks and references to Appendices
January 12th/15 BETHUNE	Two Ford Motor Ambulance wagons, and one Sunbeam Motor Ambulance wagon arrived to be permanently attached to unit one other Ford wagon and repair wagon promised No of sick = 59. No 1371 Corpl March E.W. } " 1/8937 Dr Kirby W.H. } " 2336 " Leech A.L. } No number. " Bailey F.E. } A.S.C. Motor Ambulance Drivers, arrived for duty No of Cases evacuated = 68	PHG

Instructions regarding War Diaries and Intelligence Summaries are contained in F. S. Regs., Part II. and the Staff Manual respectively. Title pages will be prepared in manuscript.

WAR DIARY
or
~~INTELLIGENCE SUMMARY~~.

(*Erase heading not required.*)

Army Form C. 2118.

Hour, Date, Place	Summary of Events and Information	Remarks and references to Appendices
January 13th/15 BETHUNE	Lieut. McCullagh went to 2nd Grenadier Guards for temporary duty No of Sick = 61. No of cases evacuated = 60	[illegible]

(73989) W4141—463. 400,000. 9/14. H.&J.Ltd. Forms/C. 2118/10.

Copy

OC No 4 Field Ambulance
V 5/3/6 13/1/15

I propose inspecting the horses of the Field Ambulance under your Command at 10 a.m. on the 15th inst

A.D.V.S.
2/Divn

103

Instructions regarding War Diaries and Intelligence Summaries are contained in F. S. Regs., Part II. and the Staff Manual respectively. Title pages will be prepared in manuscript.

WAR DIARY

or

~~INTELLIGENCE SUMMARY.~~

(Erase heading not required.)

Army Form C. 2118.

Hour, Date, Place	Summary of Events and Information	Remarks and references to Appendices
January 14th /15 BETHUNE	C bearer Sub Division under Captn Boyce and Lieut. Murphy left at 3 pm to take up their old billets, the advanced dressing station and collecting point in front of LE-TOURET, they took with them two medical store carts, one water cart, one G. S. Wagon containing rations and officers baggage. Wire to A.D.M.S. re departure. No of sick = 34 No of cases evacuated 56	PMG.

(73989) W4141—463. 400,000. 9/14. H.&J.Ltd. Forms/C. 2118/10.

Instructions regarding War Diaries and Intelligence Summaries are contained in F. S. Regs., Part II. and the Staff Manual respectively. Title pages will be prepared in manuscript.

Army Form C. 2118. 7

WAR DIARY
or
INTELLIGENCE SUMMARY.
(Erase heading not required.)

Hour, Date, Place	Summary of Events and Information	Remarks and references to Appendices
January 15th/15. BETHUNE	Sergt Garnier sent out to help with sanitation at advanced dressing station.	
	One more Ford Motor Ambulance and repair Car arrived and taken on strength	
	Visit from Major Genl. Horne commanding 2nd Division, who came with A.D.M.S.	
	No of Sick = 32.	
	The horses of this unit inspected by A.D.V.S. 2nd Division	
	No 018939 Dr. Elson F. / " 1098 Dr. Fenton S } A.S.C. Motor Ambulance Drivers arrived for duty	
	No of cases evacuated 57	

Instructions regarding War Diaries and Intelligence Summaries are contained in F. S. Regs., Part II. and the Staff Manual respectively. Title pages will be prepared in manuscript.

WAR DIARY
or
INTELLIGENCE SUMMARY.
(*Erase heading not required.*)

Army Form C. 2118.

Hour, Date, Place	Summary of Events and Information	Remarks and references to Appendices
January. 16th/15. BETHUNE	Collecting point taken over by Regimental Medical Officers. Use of paraffin said to be excessive by authorities. Enquiry instituted at request of D.A.D.M.S. 15 Self inflicted wounds in at present - not to be sent down till sentence passed - also Confidential memo about them. No of sick = 22 No of Cases evacuated = 24	PHLJ.

(73989) W4141—463. 400,000. 9/14. H.&J.Ltd. Forms/C. 2118/10.

Army Form C. 2118.

Instructions regarding War Diaries and Intelligence Summaries are contained in F. S. Regs., Part II. and the Staff Manual respectively. Title pages will be prepared in manuscript.

WAR DIARY
or
~~INTELLIGENCE SUMMARY.~~
(Erase heading not required.)

Hour, Date, Place	Summary of Events and Information	Remarks and references to Appendices
January 17th/15 BETHUNE.	Visit from A.D.M.S. and D.A.D.M.S. Private Garrett 1st Kings Regiment, stated he was brother of "Lord Petrie" and that he had a Commission in the Mexican Army. He also stated that he would return to any unit except his own. Sent back to his own as fit for duty. There ~~are~~ now two cases of measles and one of suspected Diphteria in Civilian Infectious hospital. One bad case of Pneumonia. 15 Self-inflicted wounds are now ~~all~~ to be kept. all of them. Officer sent up with Electric battery by car to treat senior Officer near trenches who was suffering with lumbago.	PHG

(73989) W4141—463. 400,000. 9/14. H.&J.Ltd. Forms/C. 2118/10.

Instructions regarding War Diaries and Intelligence Summaries are contained in F. S. Regs., Part II. and the Staff Manual respectively. Title pages will be prepared in manuscript.

WAR DIARY
or
~~INTELLIGENCE~~ SUMMARY.
(Erase heading not required.)

Army Form C. 2118.

Hour, Date, Place	Summary of Events and Information	Remarks and references to Appendices
January 17th/15 Continued BETHUNE	Investigation ordered re Paraffin oil resulted as follows:- Isolated that 20 Gallons per week were necessary at present for the Unit	PAG.
	Recommendations re "Swollen feet" sent to ADMS as result of Lieut Murphy's work.	
	No of sick - 28	
	No 437 Pte Page R appointed L/corpl	
	No 438 Shoeing Smith Hughes (A.S.C) joined for duty	
	No of cases evacuated = 41	

(73989) W4141—463. 400,000. 9/14. H.&J.Ltd. Forms/C. 2118/10.

Army Form C. 2118.

Instructions regarding War Diaries and Intelligence Summaries are contained in F. S. Regs., Part II. and the Staff Manual respectively. Title pages will be prepared in manuscript.

WAR DIARY
or
~~INTELLIGENCE SUMMARY~~.

(*Erase heading not required.*)

Hour, Date, Place	Summary of Events and Information	Remarks and references to Appendices
January 18th/15 BETHUNE	No of sick = 15. No of Cases evacuated = 4	PHJ.

(73989) W4141—463. 400,000. 9/14. H.&J.Ltd. Forms/C. 2118/10.

Instructions regarding War Diaries and Intelligence Summaries are contained in F.S. Regs., Part II. and the Staff Manual respectively. Title pages will be prepared in manuscript.

WAR DIARY

or

~~INTELLIGENCE SUMMARY.~~

(Erase heading not required.)

Army Form C. 2118.

Hour, Date, Place	Summary of Events and Information	Remarks and references to Appendices
January 19th/15 BETHUNE	The correspondence seems to have increased to twice the amount the last two or three weeks.	
	Visit from Major General Munro. commanding First Army Corps.	RHG
	Colonel Conway-Gordon, 2nd Division staff admitted to dressing station said to be suffering from appendicitis. He was evacuated with a view to operation.	
	Complaint about men having lost coats + boots on leaving hospital.	
	Memo to A.D.M.S. to say that the men were quite satisfied on leaving hospital.	
	It is possible that the men reckon on getting one from Field Ambulance. In future we will get a signature from men on leaving dressing station.	

Army Form C. 2118.

Instructions regarding War Diaries and Intelligence Summaries are contained in F. S. Regs., Part II. and the Staff Manual respectively. Title pages will be prepared in manuscript.

WAR DIARY
or
~~INTELLIGENCE SUMMARY.~~
(Erase heading not required.)

Hour, Date, Place	Summary of Events and Information	Remarks and references to Appendices
January 19th/15 BETHUNE Contd	The question of safeguarding of valuables has again arisen of casualties & sick. Memo to A.D.M.S. asking for ruling regarding this, as to what shall be done was withheld for a time. It is impossible to carry a safe on G.S. Wagon this would appear to be part of the large question re organisation of Field Ambulances which must sometime or other be considered in view of what they are required to do at the present day. Major General Munro G.O.C. 1st Army Corps visited Dressing Station. He suggested that we should obtain bedsteads for all patients. Will refer to A.D.M.S. for settlement.	PAG.

(73989) W4141—463. 400,000. 9/14. H.&J.Ltd. Forms/C. 2118/10.

Instructions regarding War Diaries and Intelligence Summaries are contained in F. S. Regs., Part II. and the Staff Manual respectively. Title pages will be prepared in manuscript.

WAR DIARY

or

~~INTELLIGENCE SUMMARY.~~

(Erase heading not required.)

Army Form C. 2118.

Hour, Date, Place	Summary of Events and Information	Remarks and references to Appendices
January 19th/15 BETHUNE Contd	Case of Meningitis admitted last night. died this evening. (No 2284 Private MACKAY I.M. 9th H.L.I Regt.); his brother an officer in the same regiment came to see him before he died. Visit from Major Percy Evans RAMC who enquired as to whether our motors were in good condition or not. He came with Major O'Grady RAMC. On being assured that the motors were doing well they went away Visit from D.A.D.M.S. 2nd Division. (Thresh's Disinfector being used for lice in clothes) No of sick = 45. No of cases evacuated = 4	PHG.

Army Form C. 2118.

Instructions regarding War Diaries and Intelligence Summaries are contained in F. S. Regs., Part II. and the Staff Manual respectively. Title pages will be prepared in manuscript.

WAR DIARY
or
~~INTELLIGENCE SUMMARY.~~
(Erase heading not required.)

Hour, Date, Place	Summary of Events and Information	Remarks and references to Appendices
January 21st/15 BETHUNE	Pneumonia case died today. Lieut. Matthews Gunshot Wound Shoulder has been worse last few days; some fluid drawn off pleura at base of R. Lung. Started correspondence to try and settle how arms and equipment of patients should be sent down to base. Order 555 d/16/1/15. G.O.C. 1st Army Corps said that they should be handed over to Railhead Commandant or R.T.O. Neither of these people exist at Railhead Station. Asked for ruling from A.D.M.S. The investigation about these Officers carried out by Lieut. Dyas RAMC.	PAG.

Instructions regarding War Diaries and Intelligence Summaries are contained in F. S. Regs., Part II. and the Staff Manual respectively. Title pages will be prepared in manuscript.

Army Form C. 2118.

WAR DIARY
or
~~INTELLIGENCE SUMMARY.~~
(Erase heading not required.)

Hour, Date, Place	Summary of Events and Information	Remarks and references to Appendices
January 21st /15 BETHUNE Contd	Lieut. McCullagh reported his return for duty from 2nd Grenadier Guards, and was posted to Bearer Sub-Divisions under Capt Boyce - Capt Howell having returned from leave. List of self inflicted wounds since beginning of war admitted to 4th Field Ambulance (53) and situation of these wounds in each case submitted to A.D.M.S. 2 Division Major Grogan 2nd Worcester Regt proposed for evacuation to-morrow. Orders re Motor Ambulances re books & time in and time out. Confidential letter to A.D.M.S. pointing out that	PRG

Army Form C. 2118.

WAR DIARY
or
~~INTELLIGENCE SUMMARY.~~

(*Erase heading not required.*)

Instructions regarding War Diaries and Intelligence Summaries are contained in F. S. Regs., Part II. and the Staff Manual respectively. Title pages will be prepared in manuscript.

Hour, Date, Place	Summary of Events and Information	Remarks and references to Appendices
January 21st/15 BETHUNE Contd	Advanced Medical stores were supplying Casualty Clearing Stations without being equipped for this purpose, thus delaying indents for Field Units. Ford Car with broken wheel sent to CHOQUES for repair and repair car reported to O.C. 2nd Divisional Train Self inflicted Wounds I Always fingers, seldom or never hand. II Never fatal, or indeed never other portion of body other than feet or hand except one in arm. It would appear to require some arrangement	[illegible initials]

(73989) W4141—463. 400,000. 9/14. H.&J.Ltd. Forms/C. 2118/10.

Instructions regarding War Diaries and Intelligence Summaries are contained in F. S. Regs., Part II. and the Staff Manual respectively. Title pages will be prepared in manuscript.

WAR DIARY
or
~~INTELLIGENCE SUMMARY.~~
(Erase heading not required.)

Army Form C. 2118.

Hour, Date, Place	Summary of Events and Information	Remarks and references to Appendices
January 21st/15 BETHUNE Contd	to shoot oneself in the hand with a rifle. III Some Medical Officers have said that these men all appear to have a "hang dog" look, and some even say that many of them look degenerate. I am not so convinced of this. No of sick = 61. No of Cases Evacuated = 58	PMG.

(73989) W4141—463. 400,000. 9/14. H.&J.Ltd. Forms/C. 2118/10.

Army Form C. 2118.

Instructions regarding War Diaries and Intelligence Summaries are contained in F. S. Regs., Part II. and the Staff Manual respectively. Title pages will be prepared in manuscript.

WAR DIARY
or
INTELLIGENCE SUMMARY.
(*Erase heading not required.*)

Hour, Date, Place	Summary of Events and Information	Remarks and references to Appendices
January 22/15. BETHUNE	Wire asking us to admit small pox case from Lahore Division.	
	The ADMS from Lahore Division wired asking us to supply him with vaccine	PHG.
	This could not be done	
	Case of measles admitted from No 1 Clearing Casualty Station	
	Case admitted to French Hospital.	
	Case admitted with Shell wound of Thigh, with ruptured bladder – operation.	
	Lieut. Matthews wounded Chest much improved.	
	Major Grogan wounded Chest evacuated to Base	

(73989) W4141—463. 400,000. 9/14. H.&J.Ltd. Forms/C. 2118/10.

Instructions regarding War Diaries and Intelligence Summaries are contained in F. S. Regs., Part II. and the Staff Manual respectively. Title pages will be prepared in manuscript.

WAR DIARY
or
~~INTELLIGENCE SUMMARY.~~
(*Erase heading not required.*)

Army Form C. 2118.

Hour, Date, Place	Summary of Events and Information	Remarks and references to Appendices
January 22nd/15 BETHUNE Contd.	Asked by D.A.D.M.S. for an officer to get up concerts for the troops. Stated that I had no Officer available for this purpose Wire from D.A.D.M.S. stating that there was a Railhead Commandant at CHOQUES and made arrangements to send kit to him daily and obtain receipt from him. Mr Dyas to go to-morrow to make the arrangement with the Railhead Commandant. Capt Blackwell to go with Interpreter tomorrow morning to interview Mayor with regard to bedsteads suggested by G.O.C. 1st Army Corps No of sick - 57. No of Cases evacuated = 62	[initials]

(73989) W4141—463. 400,000. 9/14. H.&J.Ltd. Forms/C. 2118/10.

Instructions regarding War Diaries and Intelligence Summaries are contained in F. S. Regs., Part II. and the Staff Manual respectively. Title pages will be prepared in manuscript.

WAR DIARY
or
~~INTELLIGENCE SUMMARY.~~
(Erase heading not required.)

Army Form C. 2118.

Hour, Date, Place	Summary of Events and Information	Remarks and references to Appendices
January 23rd/15 BETHUNE	Visit from Brigade Major 4th (Guards) Brigade. Ford Car returned from CHOQUES repaired but repair car was left behind. I sent out a Corpl. R.A.M.C. and Ford Car to bring back the repair car. Pte Burt asked to go home on leave. Applied to ADMS for telegram to go through for him as he could not have permission. Circular came out today from 1st Army giving permission to one private from a Field Ambulance to go on leave weekly. Applied for Pte Burt but numbers were already made up for this week	[illegible initials]

(73989) W4141—463. 400,000. 9/14. H.&J.Ltd. Forms/C. 2118/10.

Instructions regarding War Diaries and Intelligence Summaries are contained in F. S. Regs., Part II. and the Staff Manual respectively. Title pages will be prepared in manuscript.

WAR DIARY
or
~~INTELLIGENCE SUMMARY.~~
(Erase heading not required.)

Army Form C. 2118.

Hour, Date, Place	Summary of Events and Information	Remarks and references to Appendices
January 23rd/15 BETHUNE Contd	Lieut Dyas RAMC went to CHOQUES and arranged with R.T.O. there to take equipment. He said he would only give a receipt for rifles and bayonets and not for accoutrements. He also wished us to keep the Arms + Kits for 2 or 3 days until we got a wagon full, and to time the wagon to arrive between 2 + 2-30 pm having sent him a telegram the night before. This is arranged for. A N.C.O. will go daily with cart + take receipts from representative of R.T.O. Memo from ADMS. forwarding question of DMS 1st Army asking what motor convoy had refused	PAG

(73989) W4141—463. 400,000. 9/14. H.&J.Ltd. Forms/C. 2118/10.

Instructions regarding War Diaries and Intelligence Summaries are contained in F. S. Regs., Part II. and the Staff Manual respectively. Title pages will be prepared in manuscript.

WAR DIARY
or
~~INTELLIGENCE SUMMARY.~~
(Erase heading not required.)

Army Form C. 2118.

Hour, Date, Place	Summary of Events and Information	Remarks and references to Appendices
January 23rd/15 BETHUNE Contd	our arms & kits when evacuating.	
	Stated No 4 Convoy and told A.D.M.S of arrangement with CHOQUES stating it was not a convenient method.	
	Captn Blackwell failed in his mission to get beds; the mayor said all the beds available in the Town had been taken.	PHJ.
	Capt Blackwell took swabs out to M.O. i/c Glasgow Highlanders for Contacts of Cerebro-Spinal fever case	
	The ingoing regiment did not take over their billets but found some new ones for them.	
	Lieut Dyas R.A.M.C posted to 2nd Coldstream Guards to relieve Captn Sinclair.	
	Capt. O'Keefe appointed to 4th Fld Ambce in his place.	
	No of sick = 55. No. of cases evacuated = 22	

(73989) W4141—463. 400,000. 9/14. H.&J.Ltd. Forms/C. 2118/10.

Instructions regarding War Diaries and Intelligence Summaries are contained in F. S. Regs., Part II. and the Staff Manual respectively. Title pages will be prepared in manuscript.

WAR DIARY

or

~~INTELLIGENCE SUMMARY.~~

(Erase heading not required.)

Army Form C. 2118.

Hour, Date, Place	Summary of Events and Information	Remarks and references to Appendices
January 23rd/15	No 14702 Pte Storey Transferred to 114th Hy Batty R.G.A.	
BETHUNE	" 3773 " Atkins do - 1st R Berks Regt	DAG
Contd	" 10242 " Evans do 2nd Worcester Regt	

(9 26 6) W 257—976 100,000 4/12 H W V 79/3298

Instructions regarding War Diaries and Intelligence Summaries are contained in F. S. Regs., Part II. and the Staff Manual respectively. Title pages will be prepared in manuscript.

Army Form C. 2118.

WAR DIARY
or
~~INTELLIGENCE SUMMARY.~~
(Erase heading not required.)

Hour, Date, Place	Summary of Events and Information	Remarks and references to Appendices
January 24th/15 BETHUNE	Colonel Gogarty left for duty ^dressing-station^	DMG.
	Lieut. Matthews is much improved	
	Col. Conway-Gordon is put down for evacuation to-morrow	
	Letter from proprietor of dressing station for Officers saying that we must evacuate it at the end of the week, as his wife is returning	
	Letter to thank him for his kindness & to say we wish to stay if his wife should not return by any chance.	
	Have another house in view.	
	No of cases evacuated = 28	

(73989) W4141—463. 400,000. 9/14. H.&J.Ltd. Forms/C. 2118/10.

ÉMILE LEMAN
NOTAIRE
BÉTHUNE
(Pas-de-Calais)
Successeur de Me HUGOT

le 24 Janvier 1915

Monsieur le Commandant,

J'ai l'honneur de vous informer que Madame Leman et nos huit enfants ne pouvant plus demeurer à Libourne regagneront Béthune à la fin du mois.

Vous savez l'empressement avec lequel j'ai mis à votre disposition les appartements actuellement disponibles de notre maison, et vous avez eu l'amabilité de m'en remercier.

légitimes préoccupations d'une
maîtresse de maison, et vous prie
d'agréer l'expression de mes
sentiments les plus distingués

Mme Lemarié

Instructions regarding War Diaries and Intelligence Summaries are contained in F. S. Regs., Part II. and the Staff Manual respectively. Title pages will be prepared in manuscript.

WAR DIARY
or
~~INTELLIGENCE SUMMARY.~~
(Erase heading not required.)

Army Form C. 2118.

Hour, Date, Place	Summary of Events and Information	Remarks and references to Appendices
January 24th/15. BETHUNE Contd	Complaint from L/Cpl of Glasgow Highlanders (L/Cpl Stewart) who is evidently an educated man complaining of great irregularities in our dressing station and forwarded by Col. of Regiment & Brigadier General Chichester to D.A.D.M.S. Answered Complaint withdrawn. 1st Private sent on leave to-day Captn Boyce came in to see me. Consultation with Captn Blackwell, Captn Boyce, and Quartermaster regarding Cookers being supplied. Decided to ask that they should not be supplied, but if they had to be supplied, we wanted two.	PKG.

Instructions regarding War Diaries and Intelligence Summaries are contained in F. S. Regs., Part II. and the Staff Manual respectively. Title pages will be prepared in manuscript.

WAR DIARY
or
~~INTELLIGENCE SUMMARY~~.
(Erase heading not required.)

Army Form C. 2118.

Hour, Date, Place	Summary of Events and Information	Remarks and references to Appendices
January 24th/15 BETHUNE Contd	Complaint by D.A.D.M.S. that our men were dirty and unshaved in the Advanced dressing station & that their clothes were torn & worn.	PHJ.
	Some new clothes are indented for on the strength of this.	
	Complaint by two Staff Officers in dressing station for Officers that food was not well cooked & served.	
	Thanked them for complaining & made arrangements for rectifying it.	
	Bladder case is slightly improved	
	No 17117 Pte Blount H. 2nd Gren Gds arrived for duty	
	No of ~~Sick~~ = 17	
	No 19108 Pte Waller H. 2nd Gren Gds. arrived for duty. Gren Gds to look after rifles & ammunition	

(73989) W4141—463. 400,000. 9/14. H.&J.Ltd. Forms/C. 2118/10.

Instructions regarding War Diaries and Intelligence Summaries are contained in F. S. Regs., Part II. and the Staff Manual respectively. Title pages will be prepared in manuscript.

WAR DIARY
or
~~INTELLIGENCE SUMMARY.~~
(Erase heading not required.)

Army Form C. 2118.

Hour, Date, Place	Summary of Events and Information	Remarks and references to Appendices
January 25th/15 BETHUNE	Town began to be shelled at 4 a.m. Four shells entered buildings of No 1 Clearing Casualty Station which was promptly evacuated Two or three orderlies wounded. Wire at 9.30 am telling me to go to ROBECQ. packed up and left at 12 Midday. All patients evacuated by No 7 Motor Ambulance Convoy who did really good work to railway station, whence they were all taken by Ambulance train. Marched 5½ miles to ROBECQ. Men billeted in farm close to Cross-roads in village	DMcL

(73989) W4141—463. 400,000. 9/14. H.&J.Ltd. Forms/C. 2118/10.

Instructions regarding War Diaries and Intelligence Summaries are contained in F. S. Regs., Part II. and the Staff Manual respectively. Title pages will be prepared in manuscript.

WAR DIARY
or
~~INTELLIGENCE SUMMARY.~~

(*Erase heading not required.*)

Army Form C. 2118.

Hour, Date, Place	Summary of Events and Information	Remarks and references to Appendices
January 25th/15 ROBECQ Contd	Officers in Farm House.	PHG.
	Made 100 beds for sick & wounded in Boys Schoolhouse.	
	No 5 Field Ambulance in Girls' School	
	No 6 Field Ambulance in farm behind this School	
	Notified ~~[illegible]~~ Bearer Sub-Divisions of my dispositions & sent him 2 Ford Cars and the Sunbeam to them.	
	A.D.M.S. came & saw dispositions.	
	Notified A.D.M.S. later in writing of them.	
	No of sick = 29.	
	No of cases evacuated = 33	

(73989) W4141—463. 400,000. 9/14. H.&J.Ltd. Forms/C. 2118/10.

Instructions regarding War Diaries and Intelligence Summaries are contained in F. S. Regs., Part II. and the Staff Manual respectively. Title pages will be prepared in manuscript.

WAR DIARY
or
~~INTELLIGENCE~~ SUMMARY.
(Erase heading not required.)

Army Form C. 2118.

Hour, Date, Place	Summary of Events and Information	Remarks and references to Appendices
January 26/15 BOBECQ	ADMS says all sick & wounded ~~to be sent~~ to be sent to Clearing Hospital at MERVILLE and a return of sick & wounded to be sent in, reporting how many sent in previous 24 hours. Bearer Division still at L'in L'EPINETTE & farm near Infantry Brigade HQrs in front of LE-TOURET. They are evacuating all serious cases direct to Clearing Hl at MERVILLE and self inflicted cases & ordinary cases to us here. The section of 5th Field Ambulance evacuated Girls School to-day.	PHG

(73989) W4141—463. 400,000. 9/14. H.&J.Ltd. Forms/C. 2118/10.

Instructions regarding War Diaries and Intelligence Summaries are contained in F. S. Regs., Part II. and the Staff Manual respectively. Title pages will be prepared in manuscript.

WAR DIARY
or
INTELLIGENCE SUMMARY.
(Erase heading not required.)

Army Form C. 2118.

Hour, Date, Place	Summary of Events and Information	Remarks and references to Appendices
January 26th/15 ROBECQ	Cleaned out Boys Girls Schools – made 200 beds. 2 Schoolrooms & 3 upper rooms in Schoolmaster's house at Boys School for sick and self inflicted Cases. Wounded cases in 2 large rooms in Girls School these very Convenient, opposite door is a large room for dressing & minor operations Upstairs in Girls School are small rooms for night orderlies to sleep in. Room downstairs will Contain another 50, or 80 if necessary later, and there are upper rooms which can be used in Emergency	[initials]

(73989) W4141—463. 400,000. 9/14. H.&J.Ltd. Forms/C. 2118/10.

Instructions regarding War Diaries and Intelligence Summaries are contained in F. S. Regs., Part II. and the Staff Manual respectively. Title pages will be prepared in manuscript.

WAR DIARY
or
~~INTELLIGENCE SUMMARY~~.
(*Erase heading not required.*)

Army Form C. 2118.

Hour, Date, Place	Summary of Events and Information	Remarks and references to Appendices
January 26th/15 ROBECQ	The orderly Officer will have a bedroom & sitting room in the Girls Mistress's house. Store in room attached to Church quite close to doors of both Schools. The cars can go right round the Church and stop on the way at both doors of both Schools. An office in a house in the principal Street and there is a policeman outside who will stop each car as it comes up with Sick & wounded	PHG

Instructions regarding War Diaries and Intelligence Summaries are contained in F. S. Regs., Part II. and the Staff Manual respectively. Title pages will be prepared in manuscript.

WAR DIARY
or
~~INTELLIGENCE SUMMARY.~~
(Erase heading not required.)

Army Form C. 2118.

Hour, Date, Place	Summary of Events and Information	Remarks and references to Appendices
January 26th/15 ROBECQ	Men billeted close to Cross-roads in middle of Village in a barn marked in diagram. Two beds for officers, in house marked in diagram. One Ford Car to remain at the dressing station & other 3 including Sunbeam at Advanced dressing station, as they have to evacuate to MERVILLE direct all serious Cases Visited Advanced dressing station in front of LE-TOURET today. The advanced dressing station is loopholed & there is a redoubt in garden & two machine guns upstairs, put in today by Engineers	PAG.

(73989) W4141—463. 400,000. 9/14. H.&J.Ltd. Forms/C. 2118/10.

Instructions regarding War Diaries and Intelligence Summaries are contained in F. S. Regs., Part II. and the Staff Manual respectively. Title pages will be prepared in manuscript.

WAR DIARY
or
~~INTELLIGENCE~~ SUMMARY.
(Erase heading not required.)

Army Form C. 2118.

Hour, Date, Place	Summary of Events and Information	Remarks and references to Appendices
January 26th/15 ROBECQ	Suggested that Red Cross flag should be removed from this building. This was done & a small distinguishing flag put above door instead. Weather cold but fine No of sick = 1 No of cases evacuated = 200.	PMG

Instructions regarding War Diaries and Intelligence Summaries are contained in F. S. Regs., Part II. and the Staff Manual respectively. Title pages will be prepared in manuscript.

WAR DIARY
or
~~INTELLIGENCE SUMMARY.~~
(Erase heading not required.)

Army Form C. 2118.

Hour, Date, Place	Summary of Events and Information	Remarks and references to Appendices
January 27th/15 ROBECQ	Went to MERVILLE. Visited No 6 Clearing Hospital and saw Lt Col Lord Rank. who said he would take our cases at any time, but would like them in daylight. Went to Head Quarters of No 2 British Red Cross Convoy and arranged for 2 cars to go to ROBECQ at once to evacuate. A permanent arrangement was made for one car to come at 11 a.m. every day & evacuate; the driver to take back a note to say how many more cars will be required during the day. No 7 Clearing Hospital also at MERVILLE will take any that No 6 cannot take.	PHG.

(9 26 6) W257—976 100,000 4/12 H W V 79/3298

Instructions regarding War Diaries and Intelligence Summaries are contained in F. S. Regs., Part II. and the Staff Manual respectively. Title pages will be prepared in manuscript.

WAR DIARY
or
INTELLIGENCE SUMMARY.
(*Erase heading not required.*)

Army Form C. 2118.

Hour, Date, Place	Summary of Events and Information	Remarks and references to Appendices
January 27th/15 ROBECQ Contd	Diagram of dispositions sent to the A.D.M.S. 2nd Division	PHG.
	No of Sick = 52	
	No of Cases evacuated. = Nil	

Instructions regarding War Diaries and Intelligence Summaries are contained in F. S. Regs., Part II. and the Staff Manual respectively. Title pages will be prepared in manuscript.

WAR DIARY

or

~~INTELLIGENCE SUMMARY.~~

(Erase heading not required.)

Army Form C. 2118.

Hour, Date, Place	Summary of Events and Information	Remarks and references to Appendices
January 28th/15. ROBECQ	Reinforcements :- 34845 Private Neasham B. / 42250 " Newman E. / 34404 " Norman F. J. / 40768 " Payne A. M. / 33788 " Edwards C. D. / 36092 " Pace F. W. / 41781 " Pegler S. / 39668 " Peters L. M. / 33871 " Spencer W. G. / 40694 " Payne A. S. } Arrived for duty 28/1/15	PHG
	The wards are well fitted with stoves and the lighting is good. Beds 280.	
	Notice boards made for medical Officers billets - Office - and Dressing Station. Flags over Office & by Dressing Station -	
	Distinguishing lights at night	

(9 26 6) W 257—976 100,000 4/12 H W V 79/3298

Army Form C. 2118.

Instructions regarding War Diaries and Intelligence Summaries are contained in F. S. Regs., Part II. and the Staff Manual respectively. Title pages will be prepared in manuscript.

WAR DIARY
or
INTELLIGENCE SUMMARY.
(Erase heading not required.)

Hour, Date, Place	Summary of Events and Information	Remarks and references to Appendices
January 28th/15 ROBECQ Contd	Horses inspected by O.C. Divisional Train	[illegible]
	Number Sick = 26	
	No of cases evacuated = 10	

O.C. 4 Field Ambulance

Lt Colonel Brooke reports that he is particularly well pleased with the state in which he found the horses of your unit – and has recorded this opinion in the report of his inspection.

The G.O.C. has asked me to communicate the above facts to you. It would be well that your drivers should be informed as it may encourage them.

[illegible]

D A D Vet. 2 D

29/1/15

Instructions regarding War Diaries and Intelligence Summaries are contained in F. S. Regs., Part II. and the Staff Manual respectively. Title pages will be prepared in manuscript.

WAR DIARY

or

~~INTELLIGENCE SUMMARY.~~

(Erase heading not required.)

Army Form C. 2118.

Hour, Date, Place	Summary of Events and Information	Remarks and references to Appendices
January 29th/15. ROBECQ	The personnel of this unit paraded at 2pm to check equipment, and deficiencies taken. Eight Motor Ambulances of No 2 Convoy did the evacuation. 5 sets of equipment & Rifles sent to CHOQUES & got receipt, owing to Motor Ambulance not taking them No of Sick 40 No of Cases evacuated = 8.	PRLJ.

(9 26 6) W 257—976 100,000 4/12 H W V 79/3298

Army Form C. 2118.

Instructions regarding War Diaries and Intelligence Summaries are contained in F. S. Regs., Part II. and the Staff Manual respectively. Title pages will be prepared in manuscript.

WAR DIARY
or
~~INTELLIGENCE SUMMARY~~.
(Erase heading not required.)

Hour, Date, Place	Summary of Events and Information	Remarks and references to Appendices
January 30th/15 ROBECQ.	Capt Boyce, Sergt Hallmore, 36 bearers, 2 Scotch Carts & one water cart, proceeded to BEUVRY and took over dispositions from 3rd Field Ambulance. 1 Division Capt Blackwell proceeded to LA TOURET ~~[illegible]~~ PKY and took over from Captn Boyce at 11 a.m; he remained there with 3 NCO & 1 man R.A.M.C. and the A.S.C. personnel of wagons, and handed over to 5th Field Ambulance bearers at 5 p.m; The Motor Ambulances with the exception of 1 Ford were returned to the dressing station & some of them assisted in the evacuation to MERVILLE. They will be returned to BEUVRY first thing	PKY.

(9 26 6) W257—976 100,000 4/12 H W V 79/3298

Instructions regarding War Diaries and Intelligence Summaries are contained in F. S. Regs., Part II. and the Staff Manual respectively. Title pages will be prepared in manuscript.

WAR DIARY

or

~~INTELLIGENCE SUMMARY.~~

(Erase heading not required.)

Army Form C. 2118.

Hour, Date, Place	Summary of Events and Information	Remarks and references to Appendices
January 30th/15	to-morrow morning	
ROBECQ		
Contd	No of Sick 44	PHG.
	102 Blankets disinfected by Large Thresh's Disinfector.	
	carried out by No 6 Field Ambulance.	
	No of cases evacuated 17	

(9 26 6) W 257—976 100,000 4/12 H W V 79/3298

Army Form C. 2118.

Instructions regarding War Diaries and Intelligence Summaries are contained in F. S. Regs., Part II. and the Staff Manual respectively. Title pages will be prepared in manuscript.

WAR DIARY

or

~~INTELLIGENCE SUMMARY.~~

(Erase heading not required.)

Hour, Date, Place	Summary of Events and Information	Remarks and references to Appendices
January 31st /15 ROBECQ	Sent for three cars from No 2 Convoy and evacuated all sick that could not be returned to duty, except 3 R.A.M.C. men. Self inflicted wounds still kept – Orders in evening to leave ROBECQ before 11 am. to go to BETHUNE. 170 more blankets disinfected by Thresh's Disinfector and carried out by 6th Field Ambulance. No of Sick = 42 No of cases evacuated = 108.	PAR

(9 26 6) W257—276 100,000 4/12 H W V 79/3298

OC 4 Field Ambulance.

Your bearer sub divisions will be relieved by br Sub Divisions of 6 F A. They will join you this afternoon and will work with half your personnel to-night. On arrival of 6 F Amb personnel you will send half your personnel to rejoin head quarters to-day, the remainder will rejoin H^d Qrs to-morrow morning with you.

(Sd) M P Holt.
Colonel
ADMS 2 Dn

2-1-15

Copy

Jany 6th /15.

Copy of message G826 d/6-1-15 from 2nd Division

Begins

In future reports the following method of referring to the front held by 2nd Division will be used AAA The front is divided into two sections the southern section A and the northern section B AAA Each section is again divided into sub-sections corresponding to the frontage allotted to battalions in the front line AAA the sub-sections are numbered from the right and will be known as A1. A2. B1 B2 &c AAA The actual sub-sections at present moment reckoning from right to left are A1 A2 A3 B1. B2 ends

For information

ADMS.

2 Division

4th Fld Amb

G 962 – 14th

From 5 pm tonight 6th Fld Amb will
evacuate new section A front from road
junction on line separating A2C from
A8a inclusive to left of present sub-section
A1 inclusive AAA Route roads through F5 and
4 – GORRE – LE HAMEL – ESSARS aaa
4th Field Amb will evacuate new section B
front from right of present sub section
A2 inclusive to road junction in S15a
exclusive aaa Dispositions and Route road
to remain unchanged aaa 5th Fld Amb will
evacuate new section C front from last
named road junction inclusive to left of
present line inclusive aaa present
dispositions and route will remain unchanged aaa
on arrival of Indian Bdes on 15th and 16th
5th Fd Amb will be responsible for evacuation
of all British sick and wounded with those
Bdes

S. M. P. Holt Col
ADMS 2 Div

104

Copy

O.C. 4th } Field Ambulance
5th }

A.D.M.S. 1st Division
Bearer Division 4th Fld Amb

Two bearer sub-divisions of 5 F. Ambulance will take over the Advanced Dressing Station at LE TOURET from 4 F. Ambulance by 5 pm on 30th inst & evacuate the line held by 5th Brigade.

One bearer sub-division of 4 F Ambulance will proceed to BETHUNE and work with bearer division of F.A. 1st Division now evacuating line now held by 2nd Brigade on night of 30th–31st Jany.

The O.C. will report himself to A.D.M.S. 1st Division for instructions by 2 pm 30th Jany. The remainder of bearer division of 4th Field Ambulance will leave LE TOURET on morning 31st Jany & join bearer Sub-division at BEUVRY.

Hd Qrs 2nd Div
29-1-15

Sd. M P Holt

105

Copy –

2 Division
R.A.M.C. OPERATION ORDERS
BY
COLONEL M.P.G. HOLT. D.S.O. A.D.M.S.

No 4 31-1-15.

1 MOVES.

In consequence of the change in the line of front of the Division, the following moves will take place at the hours stated:-

A Tent Division. No 4 F Amb: will open in Civil and Military Hospital BETHUNE at 10 A.M. Feb. 3rd taking over the part of the building now occupied by No 3 F. Amb.

B. Tent Division No 5. F. Amb: will open in the ECOLE JULES FERRY. BETHUNE at 10 A.M. on Feb: 2nd taking over that building from No 1 F. Amb:

C. Tent Division No 6 F. Amb: will take over the bathing and washing establishment SEMINAIRE St WAAST from No 2

P.T.O.

106

F.AMB: at 10 A.M. Feb 2nd.
Accommodation for 30 cases of Scabies will also be provided for.

D The remainder of Bearer Sub-Division No 4 F.AMB: will join the Bearer Section of that Unit at Brewery at 9. A.M. 3rd Feb 15.

ACKNOWLEDGE

Sgnd J S Irvine
MAJOR.
R.A.M.C.
D.A.D.M.S. 2 Div.

Head Qrs.
2nd Division
31-1-15

107

AFTER ORDERS 31-1-15.

3

I Nos 4 and 6 FLD. AMBCS: will vacate ROBECQ by 11 AM tomorrow and proceed as follows:—

No 4 F. AMB: to temporary billets in ECOLE-JULES-FERRY, BETHUNE.

No 6 F. AMB: to temporary billets in VENDIN-LEZ-BETHUNE taking up those vacated by MEERUT F. AMB.

2 The Bearer Sub-Division of 5 F. AMB: will hand over the advanced dressing station at LE TOURET & RUE DE L'EPINETTE by 4 PM tomorrow 1st Feb: to No 113 Indian F. AMB:-

The O.C. Bearer Division 5 F. AMB: will give O.C. 113 I. F. AMB: all the information he can regarding the area in occupation, also guides should these be required.

P.T.O.

Further orders will be issued as to dispositions of Br. Sect. Div: No 5 F. AMB: after landing over is completed.

(Sgd) T. S. Irvine
Major CAMC
D.A.D.M.S.
2 Div

8-30 pm.

109

Operations

December 30th.

Capt. Follett. Wound in Calf - carbolised & irrigated - Tube put in.

January 2nd

Sgt. Jones. G.S.W. Skull and Brain - Explored & some fragments of Skull removed - Extensive fractures found. Patient died 12 hours later.

January 4th.

Pte. Brown - Acute Appendicitis - Appendicectomy

January 3rd to 16th.

6 operations for G.S.W. of Brain
3 Deaths.
3 Evacuated.
4 operations for G.S.W. compound fractures of Long Bones
1 operation for G.S.W. of Urethra.

January 20th.

Pte. Bradshaw. Trephined for gutter fracture with compression.

Diagram of dispositions at ROBECQ.

GIRLS' School
150 Beds

Boys' School
Sick Beds 66

School Ho
Sick Beds 34

Church.

Qr Mrs Store

Wagons.

LILLERS

St. VENANT

Men's Billet.

2 Beds
Officer's Dressing Station.

BETHUNE

Office

Officers Billet.

121/4655
Feb. 1915

121/4655.

AMD

No 4. Field Ambulance

Vol VII

Feb.

16 Ops.

Brain – 11 – Evac 7
– Died – 4

Amput – 3 – arm 2
– leg 1

abdomen – 1

Eye – 1.

28

Instructions regarding War Diaries and Intelligence Summaries are contained in F. S. Regs., Part II. and the Staff Manual respectively. Title pages will be prepared in manuscript.

WAR DIARY

or

~~INTELLIGENCE SUMMARY.~~

(*Erase heading not required.*)

Army Form C. 2118.

Hour, Date, Place	Summary of Events and Information	Remarks and references to Appendices
ROBECQ February 1st/15	Sent 3 G.S. Wagons with Stores at 5.30 am. To leave stores in Civil Hospital where we have orders to open a dressing station at 10 am. on Feb 3rd. Paraded at 10.15 am. and marched away at 10.30 am. Two sick officers left in Ford Car at 10.30 am. Lieut. Lovell saw them off. Sent in Lieut. Morton + Interpreter to secure our former Officers dressing station and the house opposite the dressing station for our billet. Left Sanitary party behind Marched into ECOLE-JULES-FERRY at 12-15 pm and billeted men in room which had been used	MS

(73989) W4141—463. 400,000. 9/14. H.&J.Ltd. Forms/C. 2118/10.

No 4 Field Ambulance

Table showing numbers of sick and wounded, by Units, admitted during 24 hours ended 1/2/15.

Unit – 2nd Division	Officers Sick	Officers Wound	Other Ranks Sick	Other Ranks Wounded
2 Worcesters			2	
2 Inniskilling Fusiliers			3	
9th H. L. I.			2	
2nd H. L. I.			1	
2nd Oxfords			1	
Army Cyclist Corps			1	
R. G. A. 114th Hy. Batty.			1	
R. F. A. 48th Batty.			2	
			13	
Other Divisions:				
R. F. A. 40th Batty			1	
R. G. A. 110th Hy. Batty			1	
			2	

	Sick	Wounded
Admitted officers	—	—
" Other Ranks	15	—
Evacuated officers	—	—
" Other Ranks	63	—
Remaining officers	2	—
" Other Ranks	16	6

Prevailing disease: Bronchial Catarrh.

Cases admitted with foot trouble. Nil.

P. A. Lloyd Jones.
Capt. RAMC
OC No 4 F Amb

ADMS. 2nd Div.
1/2/15

Instructions regarding War Diaries and Intelligence Summaries are contained in F. S. Regs., Part II and the Staff Manual respectively. Title pages will be prepared in manuscript.

WAR DIARY
or
INTELLIGENCE SUMMARY.
(Erase heading not required.)

Army Form C. 2118.

Hour, Date, Place	Summary of Events and Information	Remarks and references to Appendices
BETHUNE February 1st/15 Contd	as a ward. One smaller ward used for Self inflicted cases and sick. No I. Field Ambulance vacated the school just after we arrived. Visited O.C. 3rd Field Ambulance who now has dressing station in CIVIL + MILITARY HOSPITAL + ascertained that he has orders to leave on Thursday Feb 4th. Wired arrival and also information given by OC No3 Field Ambulance to A.D.M.S. 2 Division Wired arrival to O.C. Bearer Sub Divisions + Brigade Major 4th (Guards) Brigade	M.

Army Form C. 2118.

WAR DIARY
or
~~INTELLIGENCE SUMMARY.~~

Instructions regarding War Diaries and Intelligence Summaries are contained in F. S. Regs., Part II. and the Staff Manual respectively. Title pages will be prepared in manuscript.

(Erase heading not required.)

Hour, Date, Place	Summary of Events and Information	Remarks and references to Appendices
BETHUNE February 1st/15. Contd	A.D.M.S. 1st Division came and asked me to take in Sick for them if necessary. 30 palliasses laid down for this purpose. We obtained a second house for Officers, with garden adjoining garden of first house. Made arrangements for billet for men for next two days in Skating Rink, as 5th Field Ambulance take over ECOLE JULES FERRY tomorrow at 10 am. & we cannot get into our new billets till Thursday next No. of Sick. 15	MB

(73989) W4141—463. 400,000. 9/14. H.&J.Ltd. Forms/C. 2118/10.

No. 4 Field Ambulance

Table showing numbers [illegible] 24 hours ended 2/12/15

Unit 2nd Div. — Officers: Sick, Wounded — Other Ranks: Sick, Wounded

Nil

	Sick	Wounded
Admitted Officers	–	–
" Other Ranks	–	–
Evacuated Officers	–	–
" Other Ranks	5	–
Remaining Officers	2	–
" Other Ranks	1	16

Prevailing disease – Nil

Cases admitted with foot troubles – Nil

P.H. [illegible]

Capt. R.A.M.C.

O.C. No. 4 Fd. Ambce.

A.D.M.S. 2nd Div.

–/12/15

Instructions regarding War Diaries and Intelligence Summaries are contained in F. S. Regs., Part II. and the Staff Manual respectively. Title pages will be prepared in manuscript.

WAR DIARY

or

~~INTELLIGENCE SUMMARY.~~

(*Erase heading not required.*)

Army Form C. 2118.

Hour, Date, Place	Summary of Events and Information	Remarks and references to Appendices
BETHUNE February 2nd	Visited the O.C. Bearer Sub Divisions dispositions I Officers billets & men billeted in BEUVRY. Officers billeted in CHATEAU on W of road in Town Men billeted in Schools on S of road turning E out of Town Square in front in which transport is parked. Schools containing accommodation for NCOs & men & about 200 patients, also for medical stores. A.S.C billeted in same building. Beds down at present for about 50 patients Motor Cars one sunbeam & 2 Fords belonging to No 4 Field Ambulance one sunbeam and three Fords from No 5 Field Ambulance, also 3 wheeled Stretchers for use of O.C. Bearer Sub-Divisions & Medical Officers in charge Regiments. These will be kept at the Advanced dressing station	MS

Instructions regarding War Diaries and Intelligence Summaries are contained in F. S. Regs., Part II. and the Staff Manual respectively. Title pages will be prepared in manuscript.

WAR DIARY
or
~~INTELLIGENCE~~ SUMMARY.
(Erase heading not required.)

Army Form C. 2118.

Hour, Date, Place	Summary of Events and Information	Remarks and references to Appendices
BETHUNE February 2nd/15 Contd	II Advanced dressing station at Road junction about 2 miles on road running S.E. BOUVRIE on the N side of the road. The Motor Car is, as a rule kept here The cellars of the CHATEAU have been cleaned and are to be used for billets for 1 NCO & 12 men for the present and 1 NCO and 6 men & also for the wounded and sick pending transport. The regimental aid posts of the Brigade of Guards are all within 3/4 mile of this CHATEAU Evacuation from the regimental aid posts to the Advanced dressing station by the wheeled stretchers & from the advanced dressing station to Dressing Station by Motor Ambulance Cars. Should the supply of Motor Ambulance Cars not be sufficient	M

(73989) W4141—463. 400,000. 9/14. H.&J.Ltd. Forms/C. 2118/10.

Instructions regarding War Diaries and Intelligence Summaries are contained in F. S. Regs., Part II. and the Staff Manual respectively. Title pages will be prepared in manuscript.

WAR DIARY
or
~~INTELLIGENCE SUMMARY~~.
(*Erase heading not required.*)

Army Form C. 2118.

Hour, Date, Place	Summary of Events and Information	Remarks and references to Appendices
BETHUNE February 2nd/15 Contd	the sick & lightly wounded, will be retained at BEUVRY until a horsed Ambulance wagon full is ready to be evacuated The wounded are being evacuated by No 4 Field Ambulance from the Areas N and S of the Canal at present Capt J. J. O'KEEFFE, RAMC arrived for duty. Capt G PRITCHARD-TAYLOR RAMC arrived for duty. No of Sick = Nil No 1644 Corpl. Flavell. C.W. promoted Sergt 255 Pte Tophill F " Corpl.	

No. 4 Field Ambulance

Table shewing number of Sick and Wounded, by Unit admitted during 24 hours ended 9am. 3/12/15.

Unit 2nd Division	Officers Sick	Officers Wounded	Other Ranks Sick	Other Ranks Wounded
	Nil	Nil	Nil	Nil

	Sick	Wounded
Admitted Officers	–	–
" Other Ranks	–	–
Evacuated Officers	–	–
" Other Ranks	–	1
Remaining Officers	2	–
" Other Ranks	1	15

Prevailing Disease = Nil

Cases admitted with foot trouble = Nil

A. A. Hayes [illegible]
Capt R.A.M.C.
O.C. No. 7 Amb.

A.D.M.S.
3/12/15.

Army Form C. 2118.

Instructions regarding War Diaries and Intelligence Summaries are contained in F. S. Regs., Part II. and the Staff Manual respectively. Title pages will be prepared in manuscript.

WAR DIARY
or
~~INTELLIGENCE SUMMARY.~~

(*Erase heading not required.*)

Hour, Date, Place	Summary of Events and Information	Remarks and references to Appendices
BETHUNE February 3rd/15.	11 a.m. informed by Officer Commanding No 3 Field Ambulance that he wished me to take over from him the CIVIL HOSPITAL. This was confirmed by D.A.D.M.S. 2 Division at 11 30 a.m. who stated that he wished me to take over sick & wounded from that moment. Took over cases from O.C. No 3 Field Ambulance that were being left behind. Posted nursing orderlies in wards to look after cases Laid down 30 beds in sick wards as a temporary arrangement for the sick. Took over all the buildings at 1 p.m. when	MA

Army Form C. 2118.

WAR DIARY
or
~~INTELLIGENCE SUMMARY.~~
(*Erase heading not required.*)

Instructions regarding War Diaries and Intelligence Summaries are contained in F. S. Regs., Part II. and the Staff Manual respectively. Title pages will be prepared in manuscript.

Hour, Date, Place	Summary of Events and Information	Remarks and references to Appendices
BETHUNE	No 3 Field Ambulance marched out.	
February 3rd/15	Dispositions the same as previously with the following exceptions that the Office had been placed in what had been the previous casualty room instead of the wooden hut, and the casualty room was transferred to an operating theatre on the first floor, also another room in the house in which the clothes were disinfected & cleaned was set aside for ironing the uniforms of soldiers in Dressing station in order to kill the lice in them.	
Contd	Arrangements made to take over the public baths which are in the hospital compound, as the boiler is out of repair & they are not being used.	MM

(73989) W4141—463. 400,000. 9/14. H.&J.Ltd. Forms/C. 2118/10.

Army Form C. 2118.

Instructions regarding War Diaries and Intelligence Summaries are contained in F. S. Regs., Part II. and the Staff Manual respectively. Title pages will be prepared in manuscript.

WAR DIARY
or
~~INTELLIGENCE SUMMARY.~~
(*Erase heading not required.*)

Hour, Date, Place	Summary of Events and Information	Remarks and references to Appendices
BETHUNE February 3rd Contd	This was done in order to comply with ADMS' order, that every man admitted to the dressing station should have a bath within a few hours of his admission if he was fit for it. When the baths are repaired, an arrangement will be made either to use them or to use a building situated behind the bakery. An order signed by the Mayor has been procured for this. The Mayor has also signed an order for us to take beds, night commodes & foot baths from the ECOLES-DES-JEUNES-FILLES. and bring them to the Dressing station; this was requested by the G.O.C. 1st Army Corps and ordered by the ADMS. 2 Division	MP

(73989) W4141—463. 400,000. 9/14. H.&J.Ltd. Forms/C. 2118/10.

Instructions regarding War Diaries and Intelligence Summaries are contained in F. S. Regs., Part II. and the Staff Manual respectively. Title pages will be prepared in manuscript.

WAR DIARY
or
~~INTELLIGENCE~~ SUMMARY.
(Erase heading not required.)

Army Form C. 2118.

Hour, Date, Place	Summary of Events and Information	Remarks and references to Appendices
BETHUNE February 3rd/15 Contd	Every soldier therefore admitted to the Dressing Station will we hope have a bed, a bath, a clean set of underclothing, his uniform ironed to free it from lice, his boots cleaned & softened his clothes cleaned & brushed before returning to the trenches or before being evacuated. The evacuation is not to be held up by any of these. No of Sick Nil Lieut T Bourne-Price RAMC (CS) arrived for duty " H.N. Cooke RAMC (CS) proceeded to St OMER for duty Capt. G. PRITCHARD-TAYLOR proceeded to No 5 Field Ambce for duty.	[initials]

(73989) W4141—463. 400,000. 9/14. H.&J.Ltd. Forms/C. 2118/10.

No 4 Field Ambulance.

Table showing numbers of sick and wounded, by units, admitted during 24 hours ended 9 a.m. 4/2/15.

Unit - 2nd Divn.	Officers Sick	Officers Wndd.	Other Ranks Sick	Other Ranks Wndd.
2nd Gren. Gds.	1	–	–	3
2nd Coldm. Gds.	1	–	6	2
3rd Coldm. Gds.	–	–	1	6
1st Irish Gds.	–	–	1	2
1st Herts T.	1	–	–	–
1st Kings L'pool.	–	1	15	–
1st Ryl. Berks.	–	–	7	–
2nd S. Staffs.	1	–	–	5
2nd Oxfords.	–	–	2	1
2nd Worcesters.	–	–	2	–
R.E. 11th Co.	1	–	2	–
Totals.	5	1	36	19
Other Divisions.				
1 L. Nth Lancs.	–	–	10	–
1 Bk Watch.	–	–	2	–
1 Gordon Hdrs.	–	–	1	–
1 Seaforth Hdrs.	–	–	2	–
2. K.R.R.	–	–	1	–
3rd Gloucesters.	–	–	–	1
2nd Ryl Scots.	1	–	–	–
2nd Welsh	1	–	5	[illegible]
2nd Ryl Sussex	1	–	2	–
1st Gren Gds.	–	1	–	–
2nd Sth Wales Borderers.	–	–	5	–
1st Queens.	–	–	1	–
1st Gloucesters.	–	–	–	1
RAMC att. 2nd Bde R.F.A.	1	–	–	–
R.F.A. 117th Batty.	–	–	1	–
" 46th "	–	–	2	–
2nd Munsters.	–	–	6	3
4th Welsh.	–	–	3	–
1st Coldm. Gds.	–	–	1	–
Ryl Welsh Fusrs.	–	–	2	–
R.E. 26th Coy.	–	–	1	–
Mtd Mach. Gun Batt No 1	1	–	–	1
RAMC att. ... Corps.	–	–	1	–
Totals.	5	1	46	7

Prevailing Disease :- Bronchitis Catarrhal.

Cases admitted with foot troubles - 15

P.T.O.

	Sick	Wd.
Admitted Officers	10	2
" Other Ranks	82	26
Evacuated Officers	—	—
" Other Ranks	19	19
Remaining Officers	12*	2*
Other Ranks	51	86

2nd Gren. Gds.	Capt. Hughes J.		Bronchitis
1st Herts.	Capt. Bevan T.		"
2nd Colds Gds.	Lieut Taylor F. G. S.		N. Y. D.
2nd S. Staffs	Lieut Burke H. J.		N. Y. D.
2nd R. Scots.	2 Lieut Bullock M. C.		Contusion Back
2nd Welsh	Lieut Bull C. E. S.		Bronchitis
2nd Sussex	2 Lieut Dicker A. S. H.		Pharyngitis
1st Herts.	Lieut Palmer V. A.		Bronchitis
2nd Gren. Gds.	Capt de Crespigny C.		"
R. E. Mt. Coy.	" Shakespeare A. T.		Synovitis
R. A. M. C. 25th Bde R. F. A.	Lieut Gill J.		Influenza.
~~[illegible]~~			
1st Gren. Gds.	2nd Lieut Hope G. W. V.		G. S. W. L. Arm
1st Kings	2nd Lieut Norman H.		G. S. W. R. Arm.

P. A. Lloyd Jones.
Capt. R.A.M.C.
O.C. No. 4 Fd. Amb.

4-2-15

A.D.M.S.
2 Div.

Instructions regarding War Diaries and Intelligence Summaries are contained in F. S. Regs., Part II. and the Staff Manual respectively. Title pages will be prepared in manuscript.

WAR DIARY
or
~~INTELLIGENCE SUMMARY.~~
(Erase heading not required.)

Army Form C. 2118.

Hour, Date, Place	Summary of Events and Information	Remarks and references to Appendices
BETHUNE February 4th/15	Major R. F. S. GRANT. 5th Infantry Brigade. – Major admitted with shell wound involving Spinal Column at level of 4th Rib behind Condition Serious. Asked A.D.M.S. 2 Division for another officer temporarily as Capt. T. J. O'KEEFFE. RAMC was ill with influenza Recalled Lieut. B.N. MURPHY RAMC (C.S) temporarily from bearers till one could be sent. Lieut. MURPHY is working out following departments:– (1) Bathing. – Under orders of A.D.M.S. every patient who is fit must have a bath within a few hours of admission & have a suit of clean	M.

Instructions regarding War Diaries and Intelligence Summaries are contained in F. S. Regs., Part II. and the Staff Manual respectively. Title pages will be prepared in manuscript.

WAR DIARY
or
~~INTELLIGENCE~~ SUMMARY.
(Erase heading not required.)

Army Form C. 2118.

Hour, Date, Place	Summary of Events and Information	Remarks and references to Appendices
BETHUNE February 4th/15 Contd	underclothing (2) Disinfection & Washing. Underclothes are treated in two small Thresh's disinfectors & sent to French Laundry afterwards (3) Ironing. Uniforms & Great Coats are ironed to free them from lice (4) Cleaning Great coats are cleaned by scraping & brushing. (5) Boot Department. Boots are dried, & cleaned; and then smeared with hot lubricating oil	W.

(73989) W4141—463. 400,000. 9/14. H.&J.Ltd. Forms/C. 2118/10.

Instructions regarding War Diaries and Intelligence Summaries are contained in F. S. Regs., Part II. and the Staff Manual respectively. Title pages will be prepared in manuscript.

WAR DIARY
or
~~INTELLIGENCE SUMMARY.~~
(Erase heading not required.)

Army Form C. 2118.

Hour, Date, Place	Summary of Events and Information	Remarks and references to Appendices
BETHUNE	(6) Rifles & Ammunition	
February 4th/15	Rifles are cleaned & oiled by two Guardsmen attached for the purpose.	
Contd	Ammunition is stored until a sufficient amount is collected to make it worth while sending it to the Ammunition Column	
	Lieut. SMITH RAMC (S.R) arrived for temporary duty at 10 p.m. from No 6 Field Ambulance.	
	Lieut. B.N. MURPHY RAMC will therefore return after starting the above ~~departments~~ at Midday.	
	Between 30 & 50 cases who do not require transfer to the base will be sent to	M

(73989) W4141—463. 400,000. 9/14. H.&J.Ltd. Forms/C. 2118/10.

Instructions regarding War Diaries and Intelligence Summaries are contained in F. S. Regs., Part II. and the Staff Manual respectively. Title pages will be prepared in manuscript.

WAR DIARY

or

~~INTELLIGENCE SUMMARY~~.

(Erase heading not required.)

Army Form C. 2118.

Hour, Date, Place	Summary of Events and Information	Remarks and references to Appendices
BETHUNE February 4th/15 Contd	No 5 Field Ambulance by orders of ADMS 2nd Division tomorrow. No of Casualties — 120	MR

(73989) W4141—463. 400,000. 9/14. H.&J.Ltd. Forms/C. 2118/10.

No. [illegible] Field Ambulance

To [illegible] admitted during [illegible] 4/2/15.

Unit and Division	Officers Sick	Officers Wounded	Other Ranks Sick	Other Ranks Wounded
2nd [illegible] Regt.			2	13
2nd [illegible]			–	1
3rd [illegible]			1	–
1st [illegible] Gds			2	–
1st Herts (T)			–	2
2nd [illegible]			4	–
2nd H. L. I.	–	–	1	–
1st King's L'pool	1	1	–	8
2nd S. Staffs	–	1	–	2
1st R. Berks	–	–	3	4
1st K. R. R. Corps	–	–	–	5
R. F. A. 50th Batty.	–	–	2	–
R. F. A. [illegible] Bde.	–	–	2	–
R. G. A. 1st [illegible] Batty.	–	–	–	1
R. E. 11th Fd. Coy.	–	–	2	–
5th "	–	1	–	–
A. S. C. [illegible]	–	–	1	–
Rifle Bde (5th Infy Bde)	–	1	–	–
[illegible] (1) and [illegible] (1)	1	–	–	–
Totals	2	4	36	36

Other [illegible]	Officers Sick	Officers Wounded	Other Ranks Sick	Other Ranks Wounded
2 Regt. [illegible]	1	–	–	–
[illegible]	–	–	1	–
2nd H. M. [illegible]	–	–	1	–
4th R. [illegible]	–	–	1	–
R. F. A. [illegible] Bde.	–	–	–	–
[illegible]	–	–	1	–
[illegible] Batty.	–	–	–	1
Totals	1	–	5	1

Prevailing diseases [illegible] Bronchitis Catarrh

Cases admitted with frostbite – 6

[illegible]

		Sick	Wnd
Admitted	Officers	3	4
	Other Ranks	41	37
Evacuated	Officers	1	4
	Other Ranks	16	32
Remaining	Officers	13	2
	Other Ranks	87	30

Capt Villiers, E. F., 2nd R. Sussex, — Influenza
Lieut Henning, N., 1st Kings, — Oral Sepsis
Major Grant, R. F. S. 5th Infty Bde, — Shell Wd R. Shoulder
ϕ Capt Reid A. W. R. E. 5th Fd Co, — Bullet Wd R Arm
Lieut Clarke S. RAMC (T) (Herts), — N. Y. D.
Capt Muller, G. G. B., 2nd S Staffs, — Bullet Wnd R Shdr.
ϕ Lieut Harrison H., 1st Kings, — " " Arm

ϕ Evacuated to Base 4/2/15.

P. A. [illegible]
Capt RAMC.
OC. No 4 Fd Amb^ce

A.D.M.S. 2nd Divn
5/2/15.

Instructions regarding War Diaries and Intelligence Summaries are contained in F. S. Regs., Part II. and the Staff Manual respectively. Title pages will be prepared in manuscript.

WAR DIARY
or
~~INTELLIGENCE SUMMARY.~~
(Erase heading not required.)

Army Form C. 2118.

Hour, Date, Place	Summary of Events and Information	Remarks and references to Appendices
BETHUNE February 5th/15	Sir Antony Bowlby came late last night to see Major GRANT and stated that he should be evacuated to base. He was sent by Ambulance Wagon to CHOQUES accompanied by a Medical Officer who saw him put on an Ambulance train. Inconvenience is arising from having Officers of which there are more than usual lately, in three places viz 2 Houses and a ward in the hospital. Search is therefore being made for a suitable building to put them all in together. Bathing, Cleaning, disinfecting & boot &c departments are now all working.	MB

(9 26 6) W 257—976 100,000 4/12 H W V 79/3298

Instructions regarding War Diaries and Intelligence Summaries are contained in F.S. Regs., Part II. and the Staff Manual respectively. Title pages will be prepared in manuscript.

WAR DIARY

or

~~INTELLIGENCE SUMMARY~~.

(Erase heading not required.)

Army Form C. 2118.

Hour, Date, Place	Summary of Events and Information	Remarks and references to Appendices
BETHUNE February 5th/15 Contd	Several Officers are being returned to duty tomorrow after attacks of Influenza, recommended for short leave through A.D.M.S. 2 Division – Very fine weather – Sun shining No of Sick = 85	

M

No 4 Field Ambulance.

Table showing number sick and wounded by Units admitted during 24 hours ended 9am 17/5/15.

2nd Division Units.	Officers Sick	Officers Wound	Other Ranks Sick	Other Ranks Wound
2nd Grenadier Gds.	-	-	5	-
3rd Coldm	-	-	-	2
2nd Coldstream	-	-	6	1
1st Irish Guards	-	-	2	-
1st Herts.	-	-	6	3
2nd Worcesters	-	-	2	-
2nd Ox & Bucks	-	-	2	-
1st H.L.I.	-	-	3	-
2nd S. Staffs	1	-	5	2
1st K.R.R.	1	-	3	-
R.G.A. 1st Sec Batt	-	-	2	4
R.F.A. 41st [illegible]	-	-	4	-
R.G.A. 5th Sec Batty	-	-	2	-
R.G.A. 26th Hy Batty	-	-	1	-
R.F.A. [illegible] Bde.	-	-	1	-
R.A.M.C. [illegible] Bde	-	-	1	-
2/3 R. [illegible]	-	-	1	-
R.E. ([illegible]) Fd Co	-	-	1	-
R.E. ([illegible]) 11th Fd Co	-	-	1	-
R.E. 11th Fd Co.	-	-	2	-
Totals	2	-	49	13
Other Divisions				
R.F.A. [illegible] Batty.	-	-	1	-

Previously Evacuated [illegible]
Commenced [illegible] - 4.

	Sick	Wound
Admitted Officers	2	-
" Other Ranks	50	13
Transferred Officers	1	2
" Other Ranks	86	24
Remaining Officers	14	-
Other Ranks	51	19

Lieut C. [illegible] [illegible] - [illegible]
Capt P. [illegible] [illegible] - [illegible]

P. A. Lloyd Jones
Capt R.A.M.C.
O.C. No 4 F.Amb.

Billets
[illegible] 17/5/15.

Instructions regarding War Diaries and Intelligence Summaries are contained in F. S. Regs., Part II. and the Staff Manual respectively. Title pages will be prepared in manuscript.

WAR DIARY
or
~~INTELLIGENCE SUMMARY.~~
(Erase heading not required.)

Army Form C. 2118.

Hour, Date, Place	Summary of Events and Information	Remarks and references to Appendices
BETHUNE. February 6th/15	There has been an attack by the Guards Brigade and Lieut. C M COTTRELL-DORMER DSO 3rd Cold Guards was severely wounded. No of wounded 45 (4th Guards Brigade) No. of sick 65	

[illegible]

(9 26 6) W 257—976 100,000 4/12 H W V 79/3298

No. 4 [illegible] 1 [illegible]

Table showing numbers of sick and wounded by units admitted during 24 hours ending [illegible] 10.

Units & Formation	Officers Sick	Officers Wounded	Other Ranks Sick	Other Ranks Wounded
[illegible]	–	–	3	25
[illegible]	–	–	1	3
[illegible]	–	1	1	[illegible]
[illegible]	–	–	1	18
[illegible]	–	–	[illegible]	4
[illegible]	–	–	2	–
[illegible]	–	–	3	1
[illegible]	–	–	2	–
[illegible]	–	–	3	1
R.G.A. [illegible]	–	–	–	1
[illegible] Hy. Batty.	–	–	–	1
[illegible]	–	–	3	–
[illegible] Bde.	–	–	1	–
R.G.A. 7th [illegible] Batty.	–	–	[illegible]	–
[illegible] Batty.	–	–	1	–
[illegible]	–	–	1	–
[illegible]	–	–	2	–
[illegible]	–	–	1	–
[illegible]	–	–	1	–
Totals	–	1	[illegible]	55
Other Divisions				
[illegible]	1	–	–	–
R.F.A. [illegible]	–	–	1	–
German Wounded Prisoners	–	–	–	5
Totals	1	–	1	5

[illegible]

3 off [illegible] duty

28 [illegible] R.C.

X [illegible] C. M. COTTRELL-DORMER [illegible]

X [illegible]

[illegible]

Instructions regarding War Diaries and Intelligence Summaries are contained in F. S. Regs., Part II. and the Staff Manual respectively. Title pages will be prepared in manuscript.

WAR DIARY
or
~~INTELLIGENCE SUMMARY.~~
(Erase heading not required.)

Army Form C. 2118.

Hour, Date, Place	Summary of Events and Information	Remarks and references to Appendices
February 7th/15. BETHUNE	Germans tried to drive 4th Infantry Brigade out of their new positions among brick Stacks. The result was that a good number of casualties came in during the day. Many of the wounds were serious (Head, Chest, & Abdomen) Lieut. C.M. COTTRELL-DORMER wound of head in frontal region - very dangerous. Lieut. J. PAWLE. 1st Herts Regt. ~~Bullet~~ Shrapnel Wound Entrance under left eye & exit through right temple. - right eye disintegrated. - vision good in left.	M

Army Form C. 2118.

Instructions regarding War Diaries and Intelligence Summaries are contained in F. S. Regs., Part II. and the Staff Manual respectively. Title pages will be prepared in manuscript.

WAR DIARY
or
~~INTELLIGENCE SUMMARY~~.
(Erase heading not required.)

Hour, Date, Place	Summary of Events and Information	Remarks and references to Appendices
February 7/15 BETHUNE Contd	Lieut. H.A.R. GRAHAM. 2nd Gren Gds had his right arm amputated at shoulder. No of Sick – 98.	

M

(9 26 6) W 257—976 100,000 4/12 H W V 79/3298

No 4 Fd Ambce.

T[illegible] shewing no. of sick and wounded, by Units, admitted during 24 hours ended 9 a.m. 5/3/15.

Unit 2nd Division	Officers Sick	Officers Wnded	Other Ranks Sick	Other Ranks Wnded
2nd Gren. Gds.	—	1	3	10
2nd Colds Gds.	—	—	4	5
3rd " "	—	1	6	16
1st Irish Gds.			2	1
1st Herts T.	—	1	13	4
1st Kings	—	—	2	3
1st R Berks.	—	—	7	1
2nd Worces.	1	—	—	—
2nd S. Staffs.	—	—	—	10
2nd H. L. I.	—	—	1	—
1st K.R.R.	—	—	2	1
R.G.A. 10st Batt.	—	—	3	—
R.F.A. 16th "	—	—	1	—
R.E. 11th Co.	—	—	2	2.
Totals	1	3	46	53
Other Divisions				
One wounded German Pris.	—	—	—	1
R.F.A. 44th Bde	—	—	1	—
1st Gren. Gds.	—	—	—	1
R.F.A. 113th Batty	—	—	1	—
" 115. "	—	—	1	—
	—	—	3	2

Prevailing disease - Bronchitis Cat.
Admitted with foot troubles. - Nil.

ev. by M.A.C. 81 Other Rks.
" 2 Officers
To duty 3 "
" " 8 Other Rks.

	Sick	Wnded
Admitted Officers	1 *	3 *
" Other Ranks	49	55
Evacuated Officers	6	—
" Other Ranks	29	60.
Remaining Officers	8	4
" Other Ranks	74	62.

* Lieut. J. PAWLE 1st Herts. Bullet wnd Head.
* Capt. S. J. BURTON, 3rd Colds Gds. Shell wnd Neck.
* 2 Lieut. L. G. LAURENCE 2nd Worces. Influenza.
* 2 " H. A. R. GRAHAM, 2nd Gren Gds. Shell wnd R Arm.

P. A. Lloyd Jones.
Capt. RAMC
OC, No. 4 Fd. Amb.

ADMS 2nd Div.
5/3/15.

Instructions regarding War Diaries and Intelligence Summaries are contained in F. S. Regs., Part II. and the Staff Manual respectively. Title pages will be prepared in manuscript.

WAR DIARY
or
~~INTELLIGENCE SUMMARY.~~
(Erase heading not required.)

Army Form C. 2118.

Hour, Date, Place	Summary of Events and Information	Remarks and references to Appendices
BETHUNE February 8/15	4 pm. Met French Red Cross Committee & received permission to make use of their hospital at BETHUNE for sick & wounded Officers. 2 Wards above one another. Upper one containing 20 beds for wounded & lower one for sick (20 beds) A dressing room & linen room, a bath room with heating apparatus for boiling water & two small wards each containing two beds (one of these for Medical Officers) on 1st floor. Stoves in both wards & stove in hall. On top floor a big room under roof where orderlies will sleep. Outside 2 flush latrines & court where incinerators will be built.	M.

(9 26 6) W 257—976 100,000 4/12 H W V 79/3298

Army Form C. 2118.

Instructions regarding War Diaries and Intelligence Summaries are contained in F. S. Regs., Part II. and the Staff Manual respectively. Title pages will be prepared in manuscript.

WAR DIARY
or
~~INTELLIGENCE SUMMARY~~.
(*Erase heading not required.*)

Hour, Date, Place	Summary of Events and Information	Remarks and references to Appendices
February 8/15 BETHUNE Contd/	Large kitchen on ground floor with good cooking range & gas stove	
	Electric light except in kitchen, where there is gas and in room on second floor where there is no lighting, hurricane lamps will be used.	
	The Red Cross Committee have put all their pots & pans, linen, blankets &c at our disposal	
	Shall start fitting it up at 2pm tomorrow	
	A lodge and two rooms in top floor inhabited by caretaker & wife & family	
	No of Sick = 108	
	No 7266 A/Corpl McNEILL T.E. RAMC proceeded to 2nd [illegible] for duty	
	No. 19485. Gr GRAHAM (R.G.A) proceeded to Base for duty	[initials]

(9 26 6) W257—976 100,000 4/12 H W V 79/3298

No 4 Field Ambulance.

Table showing numbers of sick and wounded, by units admitted during 24 hours ended 9 am 9/3/15.

No 1 2nd Division	Officers Sick	Officers Wounded	Other Ranks Sick	Other Ranks Wounded
2nd Grenadier Guards	—	1	2	2
1st Irish Guards	—	—	1	—
2nd Coldstream Guards	—	—	1	2
3rd Coldstream "	1	—	3	2
1st Herts	—	—	3	7
1st R. Berks	—	—	—	4
1st Kings	—	—	2	3
2nd Worcesters	—	—	1	3
2nd S. Staffs	—	—	1	3
2nd R. Inniskilling Fus	—	—	—	1
1st K.R.R.	—	—	—	3
R.G.A. 1st [illegible]	—	—	1	—
[illegible]	—	—	1	—
[illegible]	—	—	1	—
R.F.A. 36th Bde	2	—	1	—
41st "	—	—	1	—
R.E. 11th F Coy	—	—	2	1
East Anglian	—	—	1	—
R.A.M.C. att 1st H.Q.	1	—	—	—
Total	4	1	25	24
Other Ranks [illegible]	—	—	1	—

Prevailing disease [illegible] [illegible] admitted with [illegible]

		Sick	Wound.
Admitted	Officers	4	1
	Other Rks	26	24
Total	Officers	5	1
	Other Rks	40	41
Remaining	Officers	9	2
	Other Rks	68	47

Evac to M.A.C.
Officers 1
Oth. Rks. 55
Duty Officers [illegible]
Other Rks 15

Lieut A. BRIGGS 2nd Coldm Gds. N.Y.D.
" " J. PEIRCE [illegible] Bde R.F.A. Influenza
Lt Col E.A. HALL 36th Bde R.F.A. Enteritis
Lieut [illegible] McINTOSH [illegible] ([illegible]) do.
[illegible] P. DATTYE [illegible] Bullet wound L leg

[illegible] 2 o/c W.

Capt [illegible]
O.C. No 4 F. Am.

Instructions regarding War Diaries and Intelligence Summaries are contained in F. S. Regs., Part II. and the Staff Manual respectively. Title pages will be prepared in manuscript.

WAR DIARY
or
~~INTELLIGENCE~~ SUMMARY.

(Erase heading not required.)

Army Form C. 2118.

Hour, Date, Place	Summary of Events and Information	Remarks and references to Appendices
February 9/15 BETHUNE	Officers taken to new Officers' dressing station from the old Officers' dressing-Stations & the French ward in CIVIL HOSPITAL at 6pm today by Motor Ambulance. Lists of linen, Bedding Cutlery &c lent us by French Red Cross Society made by Quarter Master. They also gave us coal. Stove procured for burning refuse, dressings &c & put up in yard outside. Latrines & urinals to be flushed 3 times daily with water & Cresol. Duplicate list of Officers in occupation to be made by 8 am daily - one to be pinned	MD.

(9 26 6) W257—976 100,000 4/12 H W V 79/3298

Instructions regarding War Diaries and Intelligence Summaries are contained in F. S. Regs., Part II. and the Staff Manual respectively. Title pages will be prepared in manuscript.

WAR DIARY
or
~~INTELLIGENCE~~ ~~SUMMARY~~.
(Erase heading not required.)

Army Form C. 2118.

Hour, Date, Place	Summary of Events and Information	Remarks and references to Appendices
February 9/15 BETHUNE Cont'd	on wall in hall of Officers dressing station & one to be on Commanding Officer's table by 9 am. Evacuation return to be prepared daily by 7 am & 3 pm & to be handed to Motor Cyclist at 8 am & 3 pm. Beside each bed is a cupboard with a urinal & a bed pan in it. No of Sick. 55 No 2575. Sgt J.W. LAYTON-FISK (BRC) arrived for duty 2614 - G.C. BRANSCOMBE (BRC) — do — 218 - L.A. DALE (RAMC) arrived for duty.	

MD

No 4 Field Ambulance

Table shewing numbers of sick and wounded by Units admitted during 24 hours ended 9 am. 10/3/15

2nd Division Unit.	Officers Sick	Officers Wounded	Other Rks Sick	Other Rks Wndd
2nd Colds. Gds			2	3
3rd " "			7	2
2nd Gren. Gds.			2	–
1st Herts.			2	1
2nd S. Staffs			4	3
1st R. Berks.			2	1
R F A. 44th Bde			2	–
R F A. 41st "			2	–
R. E. (Lowland) 1 Fd Co.			–	1
9th H. L. I.			–	1
R. E. (East Ang)			1	–
R. E. 11th Fd. Co			–	1
RAMC (5th Fd. Ambce)			1	–
R. E. 1st Fd. Co.				
Totals.			26	13
Other Divs				
2nd Queens.			1	1
R. G. A. M. B. (Indian)			2	–
			3	1

Prevailing Disease Bronchitis Catarrhal
No admitted with foot troubles. 1.

Evac. to No 7. M. A. C.:
Officers 5
Other Rks. 40.
To Duty. Officers – Nil
Other Rks 9.

		S.	W.
Admitted	Officers	–	–
"	Other Rks.	29	14
Evac^d	Officers	4	1
"	Other Rks.	29	20
Remaining	Officers	6	2
"	Other Rks.	70	38

P. A. Lloyd Jones
Capt RAMC
OC No 4 Fd Amb

A.D.M.S. 2nd Div.

Army Form C. 2118.

Instructions regarding War Diaries and Intelligence Summaries are contained in F. S. Regs., Part II. and the Staff Manual respectively. Title pages will be prepared in manuscript.

WAR DIARY

or

~~INTELLIGENCE SUMMARY.~~

(Erase heading not required.)

Hour, Date, Place	Summary of Events and Information	Remarks and references to Appendices
BETHUNE. February 10/15	A.D.M.S. 2 Division inspected Officers' dressing station	
	No of Sick – 43.	
	Lieut. F.E.S. Willis, RAMC arrived for temporary duty	

(9 26 6) W 257—976 100,000 4/12 H W V 79/3298

No. 4 Field Ambulance.

Table shewing no. of sick and wounded admitted, by Units during 24 hours ended 9am. 11/2/15.

Unit, 2nd Divn.	Officers Sick	Officers Wndd.	Other Ranks Sick	Other Ranks Wndd.
2nd Grenadier Guards.	1	–	9	–
3rd Coldstream Guards.	–	–	4	6
1st. Irish Guards.	–	–	1	2
1st. Herts.	1	–	8	–
1st Ryl Berks.	–	–	4	4
1st. K. R. R.	–	–	1	–
2nd Sth Staffs.	–	–	4	3
9th H L I.	–	–	–	1
R F A. 34th. Bde	–	–	2	–
R G A. 35th Hy. Batty.	–	–	1	
Totals.	2	–	34	16
Other Divs.				
R F A 60th Batty	–	–	2	–

Prevailing Disease. Bronchitis Catarrh.
No. admitted with foot troubles. Nil.

	Sick	Wndd.
Admitted Officers	2	–
" Other Rks.	36	16
Evacuated Officers	1	–
" Other Rks.	29	17
Remaining Officers	7	2
" Other Rks.	75	37

Evacd. by M. A. C.
Officers – Nil
Other Rks. 40

To Duty –
Officers 1
Other Rks. 6

Major E. MONTAGUE-JONES, 1st. Herts. (T) Influenza.
Lieut F. G. MARSHALL, 2nd Gren.dr Guards. Influenza.

J. S. Dunkworth

Capt RAMC

for O.C. No. 4 Fd Amb.
absent on duties

A.D.M.S. 2nd Div.

Army Form C. 2118.

WAR DIARY
or
~~INTELLIGENCE SUMMARY~~.
(Erase heading not required.)

Instructions regarding War Diaries and Intelligence Summaries are contained in F. S. Regs., Part II. and the Staff Manual respectively. Title pages will be prepared in manuscript.

Hour, Date, Place	Summary of Events and Information	Remarks and references to Appendices
BETHUNE February 11/15.	Visited billets of Bearers, Officers Billets of bearer Sub Division, ward for sick and wagon depôt at BEUVRY; also advanced dressing station previously described, in CHATEAU just off LA BASSEE road and the two Regimental aid posts of Guards' Brigade situated one on road just behind CHATEAU & one in CUINCHY village The Medical Officers i/c Regiments of Guards' Brigade working in couples and are back in farmhouses No of Sick – 54	MD.

(9 26 6) W257—976 100,000 4/12 H W V 79/3298

No 4 Field Ambulance

Table shewing numbers of sick and wounded admitted, by unit during 24 hours ended 9 am 12/7/15.

Unit. 2nd Division	Officers Sick	Officers Wndd.	Other Ranks Sick	Other Ranks Wndd.
2nd Grenadier Guards.	–	–	1	6
2nd Coldstream Guards	2	–	5	2
3rd Coldstream "	–	–	1	5
1st Herts.	–	–	10	–
1st Irish Guards.	–	1	–	–
2nd South Staffs.	1	–	3	2
1st K.R.R.	–	–	–	2
1st Kings	–	–	2	–
1st Ryl Berks.	–	–	3	2
2nd Cycle Corps.	–	–	1	–
9th H.L.I.	–	–	–	1
R.F.A. 50th Batty	–	–	1	–
R.G.A. No 7 Mtn. Batty	–	–	1	–
R.E. (Lowland) 1. F.D. Co.	–	–	1	–
R.E. (East Anglian).	–	–	1	–
Totals	3	1	30	10
Other Divisions				
2nd Irish Gds.	–	–	1	–
1st Queens	–	–	1	–
	–	–	2	–

Prevailing disease Bronchial Catarrh.
No admitted with foot troubles 5.

Evac. by M.A.C.
Other Rks. 30

To Duty –
Other Rks. 19

		Sick	Wndd.
Admitted	Officers	3	1
"	Other Rks.	32	20
Evac.d	Officers	–	–
"	Other Rks.	35	14.
Remaining	Officers	10	3
	Other Rks.	72	32.

Capt. G. DARRELL, 2nd Coldst. Gds, Frontal Sinus Inf.n of.
Lieut H.J. BURKE, 2nd S. Staffs, Neurasthenia.
" H. HARMSWORTH, 1st Irish Gds, Shell wnd R. Arm
" A.M. RAMSAY, 2nd Coldst. Gds. N.Y.D.

P.A. Lloyd Jones
Capt. RAMC
OC No 4 Fd Amb.

A.D.M.S. 2nd Division

Army Form C. 2118.

Instructions regarding War Diaries and Intelligence Summaries are contained in F. S. Regs., Part II. and the Staff Manual respectively. Title pages will be prepared in manuscript.

WAR DIARY
or
~~INTELLIGENCE SUMMARY.~~
(Erase heading not required.)

Hour, Date, Place	Summary of Events and Information	Remarks and references to Appendices
BETHUNE February 12th/15	No 13418 Pte PERRYMAN A. 3 Coy 2 Gren Gds:- Case of Cerebro-Spinal-Meningitis - Cerebro-Spinal fluid drawn off & found to be turbid - Saved for examination: Pathologist - Capt GRAY. RAMC informed A.D.M.S. 2nd Division informed MO i/c 2/Grenadier Guards informed No 7 Motor Ambulance Convoy informed and asked for ambulance wagon - Man looks like dying already. Lieut. Pawle 1/Herts Regt. bullet entered under left eye, destroyed right eye & emerged through right temple - T103° otherwise doing well No of Sick = 54.	

(9 26 6) W 257—976 100,000 4/12 H W V 79/3298

No 4 Field Ambulance

Total [illegible] [illegible] [illegible] by [illegible] [illegible] 12/3/15

[illegible] Division	Officers		Other Ranks	
Grenadier Guards			[illegible]	1
[illegible]			1	3
[illegible]			1	–
[illegible]			8	2
[illegible]			10	–
H.R.R.			–	–
R. Berks.			6	2
Kings			–	3
[illegible] Staffs			2	2
[illegible]			1	–
[illegible]			1	–
[illegible]			1	–
[illegible]			3	–
[illegible]			2	–
([illegible]) [illegible]			1	–
Totals			[illegible]	14
Other [illegible]				
[illegible]			2	–
[illegible]			1	–
Totals			3	–

[illegible] [illegible] [illegible]
[illegible] [illegible] [illegible] [illegible] 1

[illegible] by R.A.M.C.
Officers – [illegible]
Other Ranks – 42
[illegible] Duty
Officers – 1
Other Ranks – 13

Admitted	Officers	–	–
	Other Ranks	29	13
[illegible]	Officers	3	1
	Other Ranks	57	14
Remaining	Officers	4	2
	Other Ranks	74	28

[illegible]

[illegible] [illegible]
[illegible]

[illegible]
12/3/15

Instructions regarding War Diaries and Intelligence Summaries are contained in F. S. Regs., Part II. and the Staff Manual respectively. Title pages will be prepared in manuscript.

WAR DIARY
or
~~INTELLIGENCE~~ SUMMARY.
(Erase heading not required.)

Army Form C. 2118.

Hour, Date, Place	Summary of Events and Information	Remarks and references to Appendices
February 13th/15 BETHUNE	Case of Cerebro-Spinal Meningitis was transferred_ No 4 Clearing Casualty Station at LILLERS.	
	Specimen we had collected of Spinal fluid was taken away by Capt. GRAY for examination	
	Heard from Medical Officer i/c 2/Grenadier Gds that the man had been in contact with cases at CHELSEA 20 days ago.	
	No of Sick = 52	
	No. 4570 Pte MARSHALL F. / 8559 " HALLAMORE H / 8639 " RANGER H. J. / 8859. " LUCAS A.H. } Promoted Corporals d/1/2/15	M.

(9 26 6) W 257—976 100,000 4/12 H W V 79/3298

No 4 Field Ambulance.

Table shewing numbers admitted, by units, for 24 hours ended 9 a.m. 14/7/15.

Unit. 2nd Division	Officers Sick	Officers Wndd.	Other Ranks Sick	Other Ranks Wndd.
2nd Grenadier Guards.	–	–	3	–
2nd Coldstream "	–	–	1	5
3rd Coldstream "	1	–	3	–
1st Irish Guards.	–	–	3	1
1st Herts.	1	–	4	1
1st Ryl Berks	–	–	3	1
1st K.R.R.	–	–	–	1
2nd S. Staffs.	1	–	3	–
2nd Worcesters	1	–	–	–
R.E. (East Ang. 1 Fd. Co.)	–	–	1	–
R.E. 11th Co.	–	–	2	–
Army Cycle Corps	–	–	1	–
R.G.A. 26th Hy. Batt.	–	–	1	–
Totals.	4	–	25	9

Prevailing Disease. Bronchitis Catarrhal.
No admitted with foot troubles. 2.

Evac^d by M.A.C.
Officers – 1
Other Rks – 25
To Duty –
Officers –
Other Rks. 13

		Sick	Wndd.
Admitted	Officers.	4	–
"	Other Rks	25	9
Evac^d	Officers	1	
"	Other Rks.	30	8
Remaining	Officers	10	2
"	Other Rks.	69	26

2 Lieut. C. DUTTON, 2nd S. Staffs. (?) Malaria and Bronchitis (catarrhal).
Lieut. F. G. T. BRISCOE, 2nd Worcesters, Measles.
Capt. R. LAWRENCE, 3rd Colds. Gds. Bronchitis Catarrhal
2 Lieut. E. L. RANSOM, 1st Herts. N.Y.D.

A.D.M.S. 2nd Divn.

[signature]
Capt. R.A.M.C.
O.C. No 4 Fd Amb.

A.D.M.S.
2 Division

Herewith list of names of the officers of the SOCIÉTÉ de SECOURS AUX BLESSÉS CROIX ROUGE FRANÇAISE who have so kindly placed their hospital and its equipment at our disposal for Sick and wounded British Officers:–

President: Mr JULES FAUVELLE
Vice President: Mr JULES BUTOR
Secretary: Mr MAURICE CAYET
Treasurer: Mr VAN ELSLANDE
Members: Mr LE DOCTEUR VOUTERS
" LE COMMANDANT HALLEU
" LE DOCTEUR LELEU
" LE COMTE de BAYMONT de SEPT FONTAINES
" L'ARCHIPRÊTRE DUCLOS
" PAUL RICHEBÉ
" DALLÉ
" LAMBERT-PROIE
" D'ALLOY
" du HAYS
" LEMAN

P.T.O.

Ladies Committee

President:	Baroness	du SAINT PASTOU
Vice Presidents:	Madame	JULES BUTOR
	"	de BRETAGNE
Secretary	"	MAURICE CAYET
Treasurer	"	LAMBERT-DAVERDOINGT
Members	"	HENRY FOURNIER
	"	d'ORESMIEULX de FOUGUIERES
	"	LAUTHOUNE
	MADEMOISELLE	HEAULME
	"	FOURNIER
	"	PINCHOU
	"	NEUVILLE
	"	DELEHELLE
	MADAME	GAUDE
	"	DISSANE
	"	DANEL
	MADEMOISELLE	CAZIN
	"	IMBRECHT
	"	de SAINT PASTOU
	"	MASSON
	"	LEISSUS
	"	DAQUIN
	MADAME	DUPONT

P A Lloyd Jones

Captn RAMC
OC No 4 Field Amb.

ADMS
2 Div

Herewith list of officials who have given us great help whilst we have been in occupation of the Civic and MILITARY HOSPITAL

PRESIDENT Mr RINQUIN
VICE PRESIDENT Mr MAHIEU
Sister RUFFINE - Mother Superior
" St LUBIN Dispenser
" MARIE-LAWRENCE Irish Sister
" ADELAIDE French Ward
MARIE GERMAINE Isolation Ward
Mr BOUCHARD'HOMME Professor at St WAAST COLLEGE
Aumonier of Hospital

P. A. Lloyd Jones
Capt RAMC
OC No 2 Field Ambulance

14-2-15

Army Form C. 2118.

Instructions regarding War Diaries and Intelligence Summaries are contained in F. S. Regs., Part II. and the Staff Manual respectively. Title pages will be prepared in manuscript.

WAR DIARY
or
~~INTELLIGENCE SUMMARY.~~
(Erase heading not required.)

Hour, Date, Place	Summary of Events and Information	Remarks and references to Appendices
February 14th/15 BETHUNE.	Asked for names of Officials of French Red Cross at BETHUNE who had put their hospital at our disposal for sick & wounded British officers, and forwarded them to ADMS. 2 Division - also names of people who had assisted us greatly in our work in the CIVIL HOSPITAL. Copies are herewith attached. Both officers & main dressing station inspected by G.O.C. 2 Division & also by AA QMG 2nd Division. No of Sick = 38.	

M.

(9 26 6) W 257—976 100,000 4/12 H W V 79/3298

No 4 Field Ambulance.

Table showing no. of sick and wounded, by units, admitted during 24 hours ended 9am 15/3/15.

Unit - 2nd Division	Officers Sick	Officers Wndd.	Other Ranks Sick	Other Ranks Wndd.
2nd Gren. Gds.	–	–	5	–
2nd Coldm. "	–	–	5	–
3rd Coldm. "	–	–	2	12
1st Irish "	–	–	–	4
1st Herts.	–	–	3	2
1st R. Berks.	–	–	4	–
2nd Worcesters.	1	–	–	2
2nd S. Staffs.	–	–	3	3
2nd Oxfords.	1	–	–	–
1st K.R.R.	1	–	2	–
1st Kings.	–	–	–	3
9th H.L.I.	–	–	–	1
R.F.A. 41st Bde.	–	–	2	–
" 34th "	–	–	6	–
R.E. (Lowland) Fd. Co.	–	–	2	–
R.E. (East Anglian).	–	–	1	–
Totals.	3	–	37	27
Other Divisions				
R.F.A. 60th Batty.	–	–	1	–
XV Hussars	1	–	–	–

Prevailing Disease - Bronchial Catarrh.
No. admitted with foot trouble. 2.

Evac.d by M.A.C.:-
Officers – 1
Other Rks – 26
Ret.d to Duty:-
Officers – 3
Other Rks – 1

		Sick	Wnd
Admitted	Officers	4	–
"	Other Rks	38	27
Evac.d	Officers	4	–
	Other Rks.	8	19
Remaining	Officers.	10	2
"	Other Rks.	101	34

Capt. C.A. GRACEBROOK, 1st. K.R.R. Corps, Influenza.
" S.M. HAMMICK, 2nd Oxfords, Acute Diarrhoea
2/Lieut R.S. HALE, 2nd Worcesters, Influenza
Lieut. C.H. LIDDELL, XV Hussars, N.Y.D.

A.D.M.S. 2nd Div.

P.A. Lloyd Jones
Capt RAMC
OC. 4th F. Amb.

Instructions regarding War Diaries and Intelligence Summaries are contained in F. S. Regs., Part II. and the Staff Manual respectively. Title pages will be prepared in manuscript.

WAR DIARY
or
~~INTELLIGENCE~~ SUMMARY.
(*Erase heading not required.*)

Army Form C. 2118.

Hour, Date, Place	Summary of Events and Information	Remarks and references to Appendices
BETHUNE February 15/15	No 1082 Pte ROSE H RAMC. proceeded to 34th Bde R.F.A. for duty. Under instructions from ADMS 2nd Div No C 142/15. Pte FRASER G. proceeded for attachment to the Div Mounted Troops for duty as cook, he will be held on the strength of this unit No of Sick – 69	

M.

1

No 4 Field Ambulance

Table showing no. of sick and wounded, by units, admitted during 24 hours ended 9 a.m. 16/10/15.

Unit. 2nd Division.	Officers Sick	Officers Wndd.	Other Ranks Sick	Other Ranks Wndd.
2nd Coldstream Guards	–	–	7	–
3rd Coldstream "	–	1	2	4
1st Irish Guards	–	–	2	–
1st Herts.	–	–	2	–
1st Kings	–	–	–	3
1st Rifle Brig.	–	1	4	5
1st K R R	–	–	1	2
2nd S. Staffs	–	–	1	–
7th H L I	–	–	1	2
R W Kent (att. 1st R. Berks)	–	1	–	–
M. M. G. No. 1 Batty.	2	–	–	–
R G A No 7 M. B.	–	–	–	1
R F A 34th Bde A.C.	–	–	1	–
R E 11th Fd Co.	–	–	–	2
" 1st Fd Co.	–	–	1	–
" (East Anglian)	–	–	1	–
R G A 47th Hy Batty.	–	1	–	–
Totals.	2	4	23	19
Other Divisions				
1st Queens	–	–	–	1

Prevailing Disease – Bronchitis Catarrh
No. admitted with foot troubles – Nil.

Evacd. by M.A.C.:
Officers – 1. Other Rks. 43.
Special Evact:
Officers – 1. (Lt. J. Powle).
Ret'd Duty:-
Officers 3
Other Rks. 16
Ret'd to Light Duty:-
Other Rks. 14

		Sick	Wndd.
Admitted	Officers	2	4
"	Other Rks.	23	20
Evacd	Officers	2	2
"	Other Rks.	56	17
Remaining	Officers	10	4
"	Other Rks.	68	37

2nd Lieut. F. C. TYRRELL, 3rd Colds. Gds. G.S.W. Abdomen (Died 16/10/15).
2nd Lieut. R. M. W. GROSS, No 1 Batty. M. G. Sectn. (Dangerously [illegible])
" J. A. STOKES, R. W. Kent (att 1st R. Berks) Shell wnd R. Leg & Hand.
Lieut. T. CALDWELL, 47th Hy Batty. R.F.A. " " R. Shoulder.
Capt. R. J. COLSON, No 1 Batty. M. M. G. Service Convalescent after measles.
Lieut & Q. M. F. S. BOSHELL, 1st R. Berks. Shell wnd R. Arm.

A.D.M.S. 2nd Div.

P A [illegible]
Capt. R.A.M.C.
i/c No 4 Fd Amb.

Army Form C. 2118.

Instructions regarding War Diaries and Intelligence Summaries are contained in F. S. Regs., Part II. and the Staff Manual respectively. Title pages will be prepared in manuscript.

WAR DIARY
or
~~INTELLIGENCE SUMMARY.~~

(Erase heading not required.)

Hour, Date, Place	Summary of Events and Information	Remarks and references to Appendices
February 16/15 BETHUNE	No of Sick = 49 No. 6218 Corpl. COCKERELL A.W. RAMC arrived for duty from 34th Bde R.F.A. on the 15th inst	MR

(9 26 6) W 257—976 100,000 4/12 H W V 79/3298

No 4 Field Ambulance

Table shewing number of sick and wounded, by units, admitted during 24 hours ended 9 am 17/3/15

Units 2nd Divn:	Officers Sick	Officers Wnd	Other Rks Sick	Other Rks Wnd
2nd Grenadier Gds	–	–	3	2
2nd Coldstream "	–	–	1	4
3rd Coldstream "	–	–	2	–
1st Irish Guards	2	–	2	1
1st Herts.	–	–	12	1
1st R Berks	–	–	6	4
1st Kings	–	–	4	1
1st K.R.R.	–	–	–	1
2nd S. Staffs	–	–	1	1
9th H.L.I.	–	–	–	2
R.E. 11th Fd. Coy	–	–	–	2
" 2nd Sig Coy	–	–	1	–
R.F.A. 50th Batt	–	–	1	–
" 17th "	–	–	1	–
Totals	2	–	34	19
Other Divs. 1st Queens	–	–	3	2

Prevailing Diseases. Bronchitis Catarrh
No admitted with foot troubles - 1

Evacd by M.A.C: -
Officers - 2
Other Rks - 38
Retd to Duty: -
Officers - 1
Other Rks. 11
Retd to light duty - 6

	Sick	Wndd
Admitted Officers -	2	–
" Other Rks -	37	21
Evacd Officers -		
" Other Rks -	39	16
Remaining Officers -	10	1
" Other Rks. -	66	42

Lieut V. FOX, 1st Irish Guards, - Bronchial Catarrh
2 Lieut S.C. TALLENTS, 1st Irish Guards, - Influenza.

[signature]

ADMS
2nd Div

Capt RAMC
OC No 4 Fd Ambce

Instructions regarding War Diaries and Intelligence Summaries are contained in F. S. Regs., Part II. and the Staff Manual respectively. Title pages will be prepared in manuscript.

WAR DIARY
or
~~INTELLIGENCE~~ SUMMARY.
(Erase heading not required.)

Army Form C. 2118.

Hour, Date, Place	Summary of Events and Information	Remarks and references to Appendices
February 17/15	No of Sick – 60	
BETHUNE	No. 15796 Sergt C. T. PEPPER R.A.M.C. proceeded to No 9 Stationary Hospital for duty.	
		M

(... 26 6) W 257—976 100,000 4/12 H W V 79/3298

No. 4 Field Ambulance

[illegible] officers and other ranks [illegible] 24 hours ending [illegible] 1915

Units [illegible]	Officers Sick	Officers Wounded	Other Ranks Sick	Other Ranks Wounded
[illegible]	1	–	2	–
2nd Coldstream [illegible]	–	–	[illegible]	3
3rd Coldstream [illegible]	–	–	10	1
1st Irish Guards	–	–	–	1
1st Herts (T)	–	–	7	–
[illegible]	–	–	8	–
[illegible]	–	–	–	–
2nd S. Staffs	–	–	–	1
2nd H.L.I.	–	–	1	–
R.F.A. 41st B.A.C.	–	–	1	–
R.E. 11th Fd. Coy	–	–	–	1
Totals	1	–	33	7
Other Div. Units: [illegible]	–	–	1	–

Prevailing Disease – [illegible]
No. of [illegible] – 1

Evac'd by M.A.C.
Officers – nil
Other Ras – 44
Rec'd [illegible]
Officers nil
Other Ras – 5
[illegible]
Other Ras 6.

		Sick	Wounded
Admitted	Officers	1	–
"	Other Rks	34	7
Evacuated	Officers	–	–
	Other Ras	30	15
Remaining	Officers	11	1
"	Other Ras	70	3[illegible]

[illegible] G. R. BRITTEN, 2nd [illegible] Guards [illegible]

[illegible]

[illegible] 2nd [illegible]
19/3/15

Instructions regarding War Diaries and Intelligence Summaries are contained in F. S. Regs., Part II. and the Staff Manual respectively. Title pages will be prepared in manuscript.

WAR DIARY
or
~~INTELLIGENCE~~ SUMMARY.

(*Erase heading not required.*)

Army Form C. 2118.

Hour, Date, Place	Summary of Events and Information	Remarks and references to Appendices
February 18/15 BETHUNE	No of Sick - 42	

M

(9 26 6) W257—976 100,000 4/12 H W V 79/3298

No 4 Field Ambulance

Table showing numbers of sick and wounded, by units, admitted during 24 hours ended 9 am. 19/3/15.

Unit. 2nd Division	Officers Sick	Officers Wndd.	Other Ranks Sick	Other Ranks Wndd.
2nd Grenadier Guards	1	-	6	-
2nd Coldstream "	-	-	5	1
1st Irish Guards	1	-	-	3
1st Herts.	-	-	5	-
1st R. Berks.	-	-	2	1
1st Kings	-	-	8	-
1st K.R.R.	-	-	-	2
2nd S. Staffs.	-	-	2	1
~~[illegible]~~ R.G.A. 35 Hy. Batt.	1	-	-	-
No. 1 Batty M.M.G. Sects	-	-	1	-
R.G.A. 7th Mt Batt.	-	-	1	-
R.F.A. 34th B.A.C.	-	-	1	-
Army Cycle Corps.	-	-	1	-
A.O.C. att. 2 H.L.I.	-	-	1	-
R.E. (Rowland) 170 Co.	-	-	1	-
" 11th Fd. Coy.	-	-	1	-
2nd Oxfords	1	-	-	-
Total	4	-	35	8

Prevailing Disease: –
No. admitted with foot troubles: 1.

Evac^d by M.A.C. –
Officers – Nil
Other Rks – 21
Retd to duty: –
Officers – 2
Other Rks – ~~[illegible]~~ 7
Retd to light duty: – 6

		Sick	Wndd.
Admitted	Officers	4	-
"	Other Rks.	35	8
Evac'd	Officers	2	-
"	Other Rks.	25	9
Remaining	Officers	12	1
"	Other Rks.	80	31

2nd Lieut. J.M. STEWART, 1st Irish Gds. Bronchitis.
Lieut. A.F.R. WIGGINS, 2nd Grend^r Gds. Influenza
Major COLVILLE, 2nd Oxfords, Diarrhoea
Lieut. N. DUNCAN, 35th Hy Batty. R.G.A., Sprain L. Leg.

P. A. Stewart
Capt. RAMC.
OC. No 4 Fd Amb.

ADMS 2nd Div.
19/3/15

Instructions regarding War Diaries and Intelligence Summaries are contained in F. S. Regs., Part II. and the Staff Manual respectively. Title pages will be prepared in manuscript.

WAR DIARY
or
~~INTELLIGENCE~~ SUMMARY.
(Erase heading not required.)

Army Form C. 2118.

Hour, Date, Place	Summary of Events and Information	Remarks and references to Appendices
February / 19th BETHUNE.	D M S (1st Army) visited Officers' dressing station No. 1951 Sgt F. J. R. MONEY - RAMC } arrived for duty from No 14 Stationary Hosp. 19955 Pte. E. W. JEFFERIS RAMC } No of Sick = 47	

MB

32

No 4 Field Ambulance

Table showing numbers of sick and wounded, by Units, admitted during 24 hours ended 9 am 20/9/15.

2nd Division Units.	Officers Sick	Officers Wndd.	Other Ranks Sick	Other Ranks Wndd.
2nd Grenadier Guards.	–	–	–	1
2nd Coldstream "	–	–	3	1
3rd Coldstream "	–	–	2	–
1st Irish Guards.	1	–	7	–
1st Herts.	–	–	3	–
1st Kings	–	–	5	–
1st K.R.R.	–	1	–	–
2nd S Staffs.	–	–	3	–
9th H.L.I.	–	–	1	–
R.F.A. 41st Bde.	–	–	2	–
R.G.A. 7th Mtn Batty.	–	–	1	–
" 26th Hy Batty.	–	–	1	–
R.E. 11th Field Co.	–	–	1	–
" (East Ang. Fd. Co.).	–	–	1	–
Totals.	1	1	30	2
Other Divisions.				
1st Queens.	–	–	10	–
R.F.A. 9th Batty.	–	1	–	–

Prevailing disease:- Bronchitis Catarrhal.
No. admitted with foot troubles. - 4.

Evac'd by M.A.C.
Officers - 1
Other Rks. 24
Retd to Duty
Officers 2
Other Rks. 3
Remained duty -
Other Rks. 12
Trans No. 6 F.A. 2.

	Sick	Wndd.
Admitted officers	1	2
" Other Rks.	40	2
Evac'd officers	2	1
" Other Rks.	35	6
Remaining officers	11	1
" Other Rks.	85	25

Lieut. H. MARION-CRAWFORD, 1st Irish Guards, [illegible]
Major H.C. ROCHFORD-BOYD, 9th Batty, R.F.A., Bullet wnd Chest.
2 Lieut A. HOARE, 1st K.R.R. Corps, Bullet wnd, R. foot.

P A Lloyd Jones

A.D.M.S. 2nd Divn
20/9/15

Capt. R.A.M.C.
OC No. 4 Fd Amb'ce.

Instructions regarding War Diaries and Intelligence Summaries are contained in F. S. Regs., Part II. and the Staff Manual respectively. Title pages will be prepared in manuscript.

WAR DIARY
or
INTELLIGENCE SUMMARY.
(Erase heading not required.)

Army Form C. 2118.

Hour, Date, Place	Summary of Events and Information	Remarks and references to Appendices
February 20/15	Inspected advanced dressing station	
BETHUNE	Mentioned in despatches:- Capt P. A. Lloyd-Jones RAMC	
	Capt. J. J. O'Keeffe. RAMC	
	No of Sick = 45.	M

(9 26 6) W 257—976 100,000 4/12 H W V 79/3298

No. 4 Field Ambulance.

Table showing no. of sick and wounded, by units, admitted during 24 hours ended 9 am. 21/7/15.

Division. Units.	Officers. Sick	Officers. Wnd.	Other Rks. Sick	Other Rks. Wnd.
2nd Grenadier Guards.	–	–	1	1
2nd Coldstream "	–	–	–	2
3rd Coldstream "	–	–	1	–
1st Herts.	–	–	1	–
1st K. R. R.	–	–	–	2
1st Kings	–	–	2	2
1st R. Berks.	–	2	4	6
2nd S. Staffs.	–	1	3	6
9th H. L. I.	1	–	2	1
Army Cycle Corps.	–	–	1	–
R.E. 11th Co.	–	–	1	–
" (East Anglian)	–	1	1	7
R.F.A. 41st Bde.	–	–	2	–
2nd Div. H.Q.	1	–	–	–
Queens att. S. Staffs.	1	–	–	–
Total	3	4	19	27
Other Divs				
15th Hussars.	–	–	1	–
Queens.	–	–	2	–
Total	–	–	3	–

Prevailing Disease – Bronchitis Catarrhal.
No. admd. with foot troubles Nil.

Evac'd by M.A.C.:–
Officers – 2
Other Rks – 39
Ret'd to duty:–
Officers – –
Other Rks – 6
Ret'd Excused Duty –
Other Rks. 3

	Sick	Wndd.
Admitted Officers	3	4
Other Rks.	22	27
Evac'd Officers	1	1
Other Rks.	39	9
Remng. Officers	13	4
Other Rks.	68	42

2 Lieut R. B. UPTON, 1st R. Berks, Bullet wnd Abdomen.
Lieut L. KEYES, Queens att. 2. S Staffs, N.Y.D.
Lieut & Q.M. A. W. CLARKE, 9th H.L.I., N.Y.D.
Lt. Col. H. E. GOGARTY, 2 Div. H.Q., Dyspepsia.
Lieut E. E. N. BURNEY, 1st R. Berks, Bullet wnd R. Arm.
2 Lieut C. H. HUMPHREYS, R.E. (East Ang.) Shell wnd L. Shoulder.
2 " L. T. DESPICHT, 2 S. Staffs, Bullet wnd L. Leg.

P. A. [illegible]
Capt RAMC.
OC No. 4 Fd Amb.

A.D.M.S. 2nd Div.
21/7/15.

Army Form C. 2118.

Instructions regarding War Diaries and Intelligence Summaries are contained in F. S. Regs., Part II. and the Staff Manual respectively. Title pages will be prepared in manuscript.

WAR DIARY
or
~~INTELLIGENCE~~ SUMMARY.
(Erase heading not required.)

Hour, Date, Place	Summary of Events and Information	Remarks and references to Appendices
February 21/15	No of Sick = 56	
BETHUNE	No. 12656 a/cpl McKEOWN N J. 17043 — WALKER N J. } appointed a/sergt with pay 15-2/15.	
	Lieut W McH M Cloullagh RAMC (SR) awarded Military Cross + mentioned in despatches.	
		M

(9 26 6) W 257—976 100,000 4/12 H W V 79/3298

No. 4 Field Ambulance.

Table showing no. of sick and wounded, by Units, admitted during 24 hours ended 9am. 22/3/15.

2nd. Division - Unit.	Officers Sick	Officers Wndd.	Other Rks. Sick	Other Rks. Wndd.
3rd Coldstream Guards	–	–	6	2
1st. Irish Guards	–	–	–	1
2nd Irish Guards.	–	–	6	1
1st. Herts (T)	–	–	6	–
1st. R. Berks.	1	–	4	–
2nd Sth Staffs.	–	–	4	4
9th. H.L.I.	–	–	–	1
R.G.A. 7th Mtn. Batty.	–	–	5	–
" 26th. Hy. "	–	–	1	–
R.F.A. 41st Bde.	–	–	1	–
" 56th. Batty.	–	–	1	–
R.E. Rly. Coy.	–	–	1	–
Totals.	1	–	31	9
other Divisions.				
1st Queens.	1	–	2	–
R.E. (Lowland) 1 F Co.	–	–	2	–
Totals.	1	–	4	–

Prevailing Disease:- Bronchitis Cat.
No admitted with foot troubles.

Evac'd by M.A.C.:-
Officers. 4
Other Rks. 38
Retd to duty:-
Officers –
Other Rks. 2
Retd to Light Duty.
Other Rks. 1

	Sick	Wndd.
Admitted Officers	2	–
" Other Rks.	35	9
Evac'd Officers	1	3
" Other Rks.	28	23
Remg. Officers	13	2
" Other Rks.	75	28

2nd Lieut. M.T.B. HOWELL, 1st. Queens, N.Y.D.
Lieut. C.St.Q. LEGGETT, 1st. R. Berks, N.Y.D.

P.A. [illegible]
Capt. RAMC.
O.C. No 4 Fd. Ambce.

A.D.M.S. 2nd Divn
22/3/15

Army Form C. 2118.

Instructions regarding War Diaries and Intelligence Summaries are contained in F. S. Regs., Part II. and the Staff Manual respectively. Title pages will be prepared in manuscript.

WAR DIARY
or
~~INTELLIGENCE SUMMARY.~~

(Erase heading not required.)

Hour, Date, Place	Summary of Events and Information	Remarks and references to Appendices
February 22nd/15 BETHUNE	G.O.C. 2nd Division visited both dressing station No of Sick = 46.	

M.B.

(9 26 6) W 257—976 100,000 4/12 H W V 79/3298

No. 4 Field Ambulance.

Table shewing no. of sick and wounded, by Units, admitted during 24 hours ended 9am. 23/3/15.

2nd Division, Unit.	Officers Sick	Officers Wndd.	Other Rks. Sick	Other Rks. Wndd.
2nd Grenadier Guards.	–	–	7	–
2nd Coldstream Guards	–	–	2	–
3rd Coldstream "	–	–	4	3
1st Irish Guards.	–	–	5	1
1st Herts.	–	–	10	–
1st Kings.	–	–	2	1
1st R Berks.	–	–	1	–
2nd Worcesters	–	1	–	–
9th H.L.I.	–	–	–	1
R.F.A. 34th Bde AC	–	–	1	–
" 44th Bde.	–	–	1	–
A.S.C. (H.Q.)	–	–	1	–
R.E. (East Anglian)	1	–	1	–
Totals.	1	1	35	6
Other Divisions				
1st Queens.	–	–	1	–

Prevailing Disease Bronchitis Catarrhal.
No. admitted with foot troubles – 2.

Evac'd by M.A.C.
Officers – Nil
Other Rks. 33
Retd to Duty –
Officers 2
Other Rks. – 3
Ret'd Light Duty –
Other Rks. – 6

	Sick	Wndd.
Admitted Officers	1	1
" Other Rks.	36	6
Evac'd. Officers.	2	–
" Other Rks.	36	6
Remaining Officers.	12	3
" Other Rks.	75	28

2nd Lieut. L. G. LAWRENCE, 2nd Worcesters Bomb wnd. Buttock.
Capt. G. C. WALKER, R.E. (East Anglian) Influenza.

A.D.M.S. 2nd Divn.
23/3/15.

P. A. Lloyd Jones
Capt. RAMC.
OC No 4 Fd Ambce

Instructions regarding War Diaries and Intelligence Summaries are contained in F. S. Regs., Part II. and the Staff Manual respectively. Title pages will be prepared in manuscript.

WAR DIARY

or

~~INTELLIGENCE SUMMARY.~~

(Erase heading not required.)

Army Form C. 2118.

Hour, Date, Place	Summary of Events and Information	Remarks and references to Appendices
February 23rd. BETHUNE	No of Sick = 44	

MB

(9 26 6) W 257—976 100,000 4/12 H W V 79/3298

No. 4 Field Ambulance

Table shewing no. of sick and wounded, by Units admitted during 24 hours ended 9 am. 24/2/15.

2nd Division – Unit.	Officers Sick	Officers Wndd.	Other Ranks Sick	Other Ranks Wounded.
2nd Grenadier Guards	–	–	1	1
2nd Coldstream Guards	–	–	1	–
3rd Coldstream Guards.	–	–	1	1
1st. Herts.	1	–	2	–
1st Royal Berks.	–	–	3	–
1st K.R.R.	–	–	1	–
2nd Worcesters.	–	–	–	1
2nd S. Staffs	–	–	–	1
9th H.L.I.	–	–	–	1
R.E. 2nd Sig. Co.	–	–	2	–
R.E. (East Anglians)	–	–	2	–
A.S.C.	1	–	–	–
R.F.A. 26 Hy Batt.	–	–	1	–
" 41 Bde AC. / R.A.M.C.	2	–	2	–
Totals.	4	–	16	5
Other Divisions. 1st Queens.	–	–	1	–

Prevailing Disease Bronchitis Catarrhal
No. admitted with foot troubles. Nil.

Evac'd by M.A.C.
Officers – 2
Other Rks. – 31
Ret'd to duty.
Officers 5
Other Rks. 6
Ret'd light duty. –
Other Rks. 9

	Sick.	Wndd.
Admitted Officers	4	–
" Other Rks.	17	5
Evac'd Officers	6	1
" Other Rks.	41	5
Remaining Officers	10	2
" Other Rks.	51	28

Lieut. A. N. SMITH, 1st. Herts. – – N.Y.D.
2nd Lt. J. H. BEVAN, 1st Herts (R.A.M.C. att.) – N.Y.D.
Capt. V. S. HOLDEN, A.S.C. – N.Y.D.
Lieut. WILLIS R.A.M.C. – – Boils.

A.D.M.S. 2nd Divn.
24/2/15

P. A. [illegible]
Capt. R.A.M.C.
OC. No. 4 Fd. Ambce.

Army Form C. 2118.

Instructions regarding War Diaries and Intelligence Summaries are contained in F. S. Regs., Part II. and the Staff Manual respectively. Title pages will be prepared in manuscript.

WAR DIARY
or
~~INTELLIGENCE SUMMARY~~.
(Erase heading not required.)

Hour, Date, Place	Summary of Events and Information	Remarks and references to Appendices
February 24th/15 BETHUNE.	Sister Godfrey - QAIMNS Reserve arrived from No 1 Clearing Casualty Station for duty at Officers dressing station also Sister - Caven. No of Sick = 26	

M.

No. 4 Field Ambulance

Table showing no. of sick and wounded admitted, (by units) during 24 hours ended 9 am. 25/2/15.

Unit. 2nd Division	Officers Sick	Officers Wndd.	Other Rks. Sick	Other Rks. Wndd.
2nd Grenadier Guards.	–	–	–	2
2nd Coldstreams "	1	–	2	4
3rd Coldstreams "	–	–	8	1
1st Irish Guards.	–	–	3	1
1st Kings.	–	–	[illegible]	–
1st Rl. Berks.	–	–	[illegible]	[illegible]
2nd Sth Staffs.	–	–	4	–
R.F.A. 47th Batty.	–	–	–	–
R.E. (11th Field Co.)	–	–	[illegible]	[illegible]
R.E. (East Ang) 1 Fd. Co.	–	–	–	1
A.S.C.	1	–	3	–
Totals.	2	–	24	10
Other Divisions.				
R.F.A. 50th Batty.	–	1	–	–

No of Sick = 3
No 19008 Serg
No 2 Divisional

Prevailing Disease - Bronchitis Catarrhal.
No. admitted with foot troubles - 1.

Evac'd by M.A.C.
Officers - Nil
Other Rks. 23
Retd to duty:-
Officers 1
Other Rks. 2
Retd to light duty:-
Other Rks. 2

	Sick	Wndd.
Admitted Officers	2	1
" Other Rks.	24	10
Evac'd Officers	1	–
Other Rks.	18	9
Remaining Officers	11	3
Other Rks.	57	29

P. A. Lloyd Jones

Lt. Col. C. A. PEREIRA, 2nd Colds. Gds. Influenza.
2nd Lt. W. S. WATSON, A.S.C. Influenza.
" " K. G. GARNETT, R.F.A. (50th Batt.) Bullet wound L. Calf.

P. A. Lloyd Jones

Capt. RAMC.
OC No. 4 Fd. Amb.

ADMS. 2nd Divn.
25/2/15.

Copy

To O.C. 4, 5 & 6 F. Ambs. G. Staff and A.D.M.S. 1st. Divn

In conformity with 2nd Division orders G 824 of 23rd inst. the following medical arrangements will come into force:-

I On evening of 25th February the Bearer Divn. of No 3 F Amb will relieve that of No. 5 F. Amb and will evacuate the sick and wounded of Section "C" on relief. Bearer Divn. 5 F Amb. will join Tent Divn. in Bethune.

II On evening of 28th February the Bearer Divn of No 5 F. Amb. will take over the evacuation of sections "A" and "B" from No. 4 FD. Amb. Bearer Divn. 4 F. Amb. on relief will join Tent Division in Bethune.

III In order to acquaint the relieving units of the area they are taking over, an officer and as many bearers as may be necessary will be left with the relieving unit on the night they take over.

IV The sick and wounded, including those of 3rd. Bde. will be admitted to 4, 5 & 6 F. Ambs. as under existing arrangements.

(Sd) F. S. Irvine.

Major RAMC
DADMS. 2nd Divn

24/2/15.

O.C. 4/5/6 Field Ambulance. Copy

Following wire No. G. 824 d/- 23rd received from 2nd Division begins:—

"The 3rd Infty Brigade of 1st. Division will relieve 5th. Infantry Bde in Section C. on the evening of 25th February under arrangements to be made direct by Bde Commanders concerned A.A.A. On relief 5th. Bde will billet in Bethune in billets already allotted by A.A. + Q.M.G. and will be in divisional reserve A.A.A. Glasgow Highlanders will remain attached to 6th Infty Bde. as heretofore and will not change their billets AAA. 26th Field Co. R.E. of 1st. Div. will relieve 5th Fd. Co. R.E. in Section C. on Feb. 26th. AAA. 5th Field Co. will remain billeted in GORRE brewery and will be at disposal of 5th. Infty Bde for work in Section B. from 27th onwards. AAA. 5th Infty Bde. less Glasgow Highlanders will relieve 4th Guards Bde in Section A on evening of Feb. 28th under arrangements to be made direct between the Bde. Commanders concerned AAA 5th Bde will carry out necessary reconnaissances from 26th. Feby onwards + will arrange for a proportion of officers and N.C.Os to spend the night 27th – 28th in the trenches with 4th Bde AAA on relief the 4th Guards Bde will billet in BETHUNE in billets to be allotted by AA + Q.M.G. and will be in DIVISIONAL RESERVE AAA 3rd Infty Bde will take over control posts in area C at 12 noon on 25th Feby AAA 5th Bde will take over control posts in Section A now held by 4th Bde on Feb 28th at 11am. AAA ends.

For information

Head quarters
2nd Div. 24/2/15.

(Signed) F.F. Irvine

Major RAMC.
DADMS. 2nd Divn

Instructions regarding War Diaries and Intelligence Summaries are contained in F. S. Regs., Part II. and the Staff Manual respectively. Title pages will be prepared in manuscript.

WAR DIARY
or
~~INTELLIGENCE SUMMARY.~~
(Erase heading not required.)

Army Form C. 2118.

Hour, Date, Place	Summary of Events and Information	Remarks and references to Appendices
February 25th/15	No of Sick = 37	
BETHUNE	No 19008 Sergt FREEMAN W. A.S.C proceeded to No 2 Divisional Train for duty	
	No 31302 L/Cpl GRIFFEN A.S.C. arrived for duty	
	No 35347 Pte LAMBERT F.V RAMC } arrived for	
	" 38839 " LEADER S.E. RAMC } duty	
		M.

(9 26 6) W257—976 100,000 4/12 H W V 79/3298

No. 4 Field Ambulance.

No. of sick and wounded admitted, by Units, during 24 hours ended 9 am. 26/2/15.

Unit – 2nd Division	Officers Sick	Officers Wndd.	Other Ranks Sick	Other Ranks Wndd.
2nd Grenadier Guards	–	–	2	–
2nd Coldstream "	–	–	–	2
3rd Coldstream "	–	–	2	–
1st Irish Guards	1	–	–	3
1st Herts (T.)	–	–	3	–
9th H. L. I.	–	–	2	–
1st Kings	–	–	9	1
2nd S. Staffs.	–	–	5	1
1st R Berks.	–	–	11	1
R.F.A. 34th Bde.	–	–	1	–
R G A. 7th Mtn. Baty.	–	–	–	1
A. S. C. 35th Co. / R.A.M.C. att R. Inn. Fus.	1	–	1	–
Totals.	2	–	36	9
Other Divisions.				
1st Gloucesters.	–	–	1	–
1st S. Wales Borders.	–	–	11*	–
2nd Welsh Regt.	–	–	3	–
4th R Welsh Fus.	–	–	4	–
1st Queens.	–	–	1	–
Totals.	–	–	20	–

Prevalent Disease Bronchitis Catarrhal.
No. admitted with foot troubles. – Nil.

Evac'd by M.A.C.:
Officers – 1
Other Rks – 41
Retd to duty:
Officers – 1
Other Rks – 3
Retd light duty –
Other Rks. 3.

		Sick	Wndd.
Admitted	Officers	2	–
"	Other Rks.	56	9
Evac'd	Officers	2	–
"	Other Rks.	35	12
Remaining	Officers	12	2.
"	Other Rks.	75	24

Lieut. L.R. HARGREAVES, 1st Irish Gds. – N.Y.D.

" H. BEDDINGFIELD, D.S.O., RAMC att. Innis. Fus. – N.Y.D.

P H Hardinges
Capt. RAMC.
O.C. No. 4 Fd. Ambce.

ADMS. 2nd Divn
26/2/15.

Instructions regarding War Diaries and Intelligence Summaries are contained in F. S. Regs., Part II. and the Staff Manual respectively. Title pages will be prepared in manuscript.

WAR DIARY
or
~~INTELLIGENCE SUMMARY.~~
(*Erase heading not required.*)

Army Form C. 2118.

Hour, Date, Place	Summary of Events and Information	Remarks and references to Appendices
February 26/15	D.M.S. – Col. Eves of Australian Medical service and Capt. Towse late Seaforth Highlanders who is blind but writes letters for soldiers, visited the Dressing station. Visit from D.M.S. 1st Army Lieut. QMr L. Jones R.A.M.C. proceeded on leave No of Sick. 67	MB

(9 26 6) W257–976 100,000 4/12 H W V 79/3298

No 4 Field Ambulance

No of Sick & Wounded admitted by units during 24 hours ended 9 a.m. 27/2/15.

	Officers Sick	Officers Wound	Other Ranks Sick	Other Ranks Wounded
2 Coldstream Gds.	–	–	1	–
3 " "	–	–	2	1
2 Grenadier "	–	–	–	1
1 K.R.R.	–	–	–	1
1 R. Berks	–	1	1	2
2 S. Staffs	–	–	4	3
9. H.L.I.	–	–	–	7
R.E. (East Anglian)	.	–	2	–
1 Kings	–	–	1	–
1 Irish Gds	1	–	1	–
R.F.A. Hd Qrs 2 Div	–	–	1	–
R.F.A. 41st Bde	–	–	1	
R.G.A. 7 M. Batt.	–	–	–	3
A.V.C. 3 Mobile Section	–	–	1	
R.G.A. 35th Batty	–	1	–	–
R.F.A.	–	1	–	–
Total	1	3	15	18
Other Divisions				
1 Queens				1
2 Welsh			2	
3rd Brigade	1	–		
Total	1	–	2	1

Prevailing disease = ~~Nil~~ Bronchitis Catarrhal

No admitted with foot troubles – Nil

PHG.

			Sick	Wnd
Evac by M.A.C.	Admitted	Officers	2	3
Officers Nil	"	O Ranks	17	19
O Ranks 29	Evacuated	Officers	2	–
Ret to duty	"	O Ranks	22	11
Officers 2	Remaining	Officers	12	5
O Ranks Nil	"	O Ranks	74	28
Ret light duty				
Other Ranks 4				

2 Lt J R RALLI 1st Irish Gds. Inflammation of Stomach
Capt H.J LEE-WARNER R.F.A. Shell Wnd Shldr Head Legs
Capt L.W. BIRD 1st BERKS Bullet Wnd R Knee
Lieut R CRANE 35th Batty R.G.A. Shell Wnd Head
Brigade Major O.H.L. NICHOLSON D.S.O. Influenza.

R.A. Lloyd Jones
Capt RAMC
O.C. No 4 Field Ambce

27.2-15

Army Form C. 2118.

Instructions regarding War Diaries and Intelligence Summaries are contained in F. S. Regs., Part II. and the Staff Manual respectively. Title pages will be prepared in manuscript.

WAR DIARY
or
~~INTELLIGENCE SUMMARY~~.
(Erase heading not required.)

Hour, Date, Place	Summary of Events and Information	Remarks and references to Appendices
February/27/15 BETHUNE	Captn. P.A. Lloyd-Jones & Lieut. H.H.P. Morton proceed on leave tomorrow No of sick = 41	

M.

(9 26 6) W 257—976 100,000 4/12 H W V 79/3298

98

No 4 Field Ambulance

Table shewing number of sick and wounded by units admitted during 24 hours ended 9 a.m. 28/10/15.

Unit. 2nd Division	Officers Sick	Officers Wndd	Other Ranks Sick	Other Ranks Wndd
2nd Grenadier Guards.	–	–	2	3
2nd Coldstream "	–	–	–	1
3rd Coldstream "	–	–	1	1
1st Irish Guards	–	–	1	–
1st Herts (T)	–	–	2	–
1st R. Berks.	–	–	5	1
1st Kings	–	–	5	1
9th H.L.I.	–	–	–	1
2nd Sth. Staffs	–	–	4	–
2nd Inniskg. Fus^rs	–	–	1	–
R.G.A. 35th Hy. Batty.	2	–	–	–
" 1st Sec. "	–	–	–	1
R.F.A. (H.Q)	–	–	1	–
" No 1 M.M. Gun.	–	–	–	2
RAMC. (att. 2nd Colds. Gds)	–	–	1	–
RAMC. (" 3rd Fd. Amb.)	–	–	1	–
Army Cycle Corps (H.Q)	–	–	1	1
R.E. (East Anglian)	–	–	1	–
A.V.C. (att 5 Infty Bde)	1	–	–	–
Totals.	3	–	26	12
Other Divisions				
2nd Welsh	1	–	–	–
1st Queens	–	–	3	–
R.F.A. 9th Batty	–	–	2	–
Totals.	1	–	5	–

Prevailing Disease. Bronchitis Catarrhal.
No. admitted with foot troubles - 2.

Evac'd by M.A.C.:-
Officers - 3
Other Rks. - 40
Retd Duty -
Officers -
Other Rks. - 4
Retd Regt Duty:-
Other Rks. 12

		Sick	Wnd.
Admitted	Officers	4	–
"	Other Rks.	31	12
Evac'd	Officers	1	2
"	Other Rks.	42	14
Rmng	Officers	15	3
	Other Rks.	63	36

2nd Lieut. F.C. GREEN, R.G.A. 35th Hy. Batty. Inflammation Tonsils.
" W.G. HEWETT, 2nd Welsh, N.Y.D.
Lieut. G.M. VINCENT, A.V.C., N.Y.D.
" C.W. DAWSON, R.G.A., 35th Hy. Batty. N.Y.D.

A.D.M.S. 2nd Divn.
28/10/15.

J.S. Murray [signature]
for Capt. RAMC.
Oc. No 4 F.A.

Army Form C. 2118.

Instructions regarding War Diaries and Intelligence Summaries are contained in F. S. Regs., Part II. and the Staff Manual respectively. Title pages will be prepared in manuscript.

WAR DIARY
or
~~INTELLIGENCE SUMMARY.~~

(*Erase heading not required.*)

Hour, Date, Place	Summary of Events and Information	Remarks and references to Appendices
February 28th/15 BETHUNE	His Royal Highness The Prince of Wales visited dressing Station to-day. G.O.C. 2 Division was with him.	
	No of Sick 47	
		[illegible]